IT'S
ACADEMIC

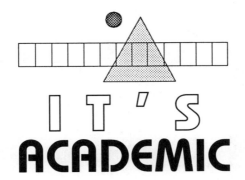

IT'S
ACADEMIC

AN INTEGRATED SKILLS
CONTENT-BASED APPROACH
TO LANGUAGE LEARNING

Katharine Schneider
Sandra McCollum

University of Delaware

MAXWELL MACMILLAN
International Publishing Group
New York   Oxford   Singapore   Sydney

Associate Director: Mary Jane Peluso
Editor: Maggie Barbieri
Production Supervisor: Russell Till
Interior Design: Aliza Greenblatt
Cover Design: Blake Logan

Library of Congress Cataloging-in-Publication Data

Schneider, Katharine.
    It's academic : an integrated skills content-based approach to
  language learning / Katharine Schneider, Sandra McCollum.
        p.   cm.
    ISBN 0-02-407758-5
    1. English language — Textbooks for foreign speakers.
  I. McCollum, Sandra.   II. Title.
  PE1128.S344   1990
  428.2'4 — dc20   89-13964
                                                                     CIP

Collier Macmillan Canada
1200 Eglinton Avenue, E.
Don Mills, Ontario, M3C 3N1

Printing: 1 2 3 4 5 6 7   Year: 1 2 3 4 5 6 7

Maxwell Macmillan International Publishing Group
ESL/EFL Dept.
866 Third Avenue
New York, NY 10022

Printed in the U.S.A.

ISBN 0-02-407758-5

For
J. E. S.
and
T. J. B.

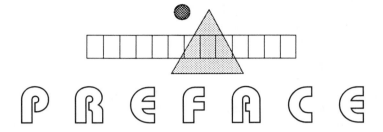

PREFACE

It's Academic is an integrated skills text for advanced international students who plan to use English for academic study. Content instruction is used to develop academic language proficiency and study skills by incorporating a variety of interactive, academically focused tasks requiring the use of English as a mediating tool. To simulate the American university classroom, the authors have integrated listening, speaking, reading, and writing skills in units from a variety of disciplines. Each unit requires 12–15 hours of class time to complete, and the skills and content are sequenced in order of difficulty.

The activities in this text are both task and group-work (student) centered. The academic nature of the tasks ensures that students use linguistic functions that reflect the cognitive operations required by the tasks. For example, when students work on a classification task, they must organize the data cognitively and then describe the classification process both verbally and in writing. Thus, both the cognitive operations, classifying data according to established criteria, and the linguistic functions, the language used to make verbal or written classifications, are integrated by the task.

The primary interactional mode for the activities presented in the text is the cooperative small group. Cooperative small group work in the second-language classroom increases student motivation, provides more input and more opportunities for students to practice with the language, and improves the quality of student talk by providing a natural social environment and framework for language use as a tool for communicating. The small group encourages students to practice and to refine conversational-management strategies. The group tasks permit students to speak out and interact verbally in an environment less constrained by inhibitions and the fear of making mistakes. In order to complete the tasks, students must listen attentively, give and request information, request clarification, and confirm their comprehension. The problem-solving strategies that students generate in their groups are essential to successful academic study.

Each unit in the text includes the following:

Preview Activities: Preview activities help students generate what they already know about the content area, forming a framework or schema into which they can integrate new information from the lecture and reading. Preview activities also help students get to know each other, so they are better prepared to work together on the more demanding tasks to come.

Content Activities/Lecture and Reading: The lecture provides new content information that will be used by the students for a variety of academic and linguistic tasks. Students develop note-taking skills by focusing on the organization of the content material, by reviewing their notes in groups, and by writing study questions. The readings provide additional content from important academic sources: the textbook and original sources. The preview, reading, and discussion tasks help students develop academic reading skills and integrate both lecture and reading information.

Skill Focus Activities: Using the content information from each unit, students practice both academic language and study skills.

Academic language proficiency skills include:

- Describing processes
- Predicting and inferencing
- Comparing and contrasting
- Analyzing problems
- Applying information to new contexts
- Classifying data
- Interpreting data from graphs and polls
- Reporting and explaining data
- Presenting and defending opinions
- Defining terms and concepts
- Forming hypotheses

Study skills treated in this text include:

- Taking notes from lectures and academic texts
- Understanding and completing typical college/university tests
- Learning how to learn and to use discipline-specific vocabulary
- Outlining lectures to determine conceptual organization
- Writing study questions to review for tests
- Integrating information from multiple sources for multiple purposes
- Integrating or relating theory to data, facts to values, specifics to generalizations
- Designing original research projects
- Conducting and reporting on research

Problem-Solving Activities: These open-ended activities require students to apply content information, language, and study skills they have learned in a new context. Many problem-solving activities are "hands-on" original research projects involving both in-class and out-of-class work.

Evaluation Activities: The end-of-unit evaluation activities focus on the typical university-type examination and include pretest review and posttest correction. The language and style of the exam items require students to learn to interpret typical exam jargon in order to answer multiple choice, true/false, short answer, and essay questions.

ACKNOWLEDGMENTS

We wish to express our thanks to the people who have contributed to the creation of this text. For her enthusiasm and encouragement at the start of this project, we are particularly grateful to Mary Kearny of American University. We also wish to acknowledge the contributions that the following University of Delaware professors made to the text's content materials: Dr. Vivian Klaff, Dr. Kenneth Koford, Dr. Mary S. Carberry, Dr. Harry Shipman, Dr. Jerrold Schneider, and Dr. Robert J. DiPietro. Special thanks and appreciation must go to Dr. Scott Stevens, Director of the University of Delaware, English Language Institute, who over the past three years has enthusiastically encouraged and supported all of our efforts to create an academic content-based course and text. For his computer expertise and unfailing good humor, we would like to thank Dave Keifer. We are also grateful to all of our wonderful students who for the past three years have "tested" various versions of what appears in this text. Thanks also go to our editors at Maxwell Macmillan, Maggie Barbieri and Mary Jane Peluso.

Finally, and most importantly, this book is dedicated to our families for their extraordinary patience and encouragement.

K.S.
S.M.

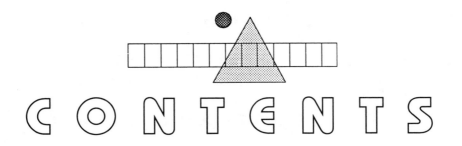

CONTENTS

UNIT TWO
DEMOGRAPHY 23

U N I T THREE
THE AMERICAN CIVIL RIGHTS MOVEMENT 1954–1959 43

U N I T FOUR
COMPUTER SCIENCE/
PROBLEM SOLVING 67

UNIT FIVE
MOTIVATION 83

UNIT SIX
THE EVOLUTION OF STARS 105

UNIT SEVEN
AMERICAN POLITICAL CULTURE 123

UNIT ONE

Second-Language Learning

Photo courtesy Lowell Reitchmuller

PREVIEW ACTIVITIES

Your teacher will divide your class into groups. These groups will remain the same throughout this unit.

ACTIVITY 1

In your groups, complete the language learning survey that follows. After your group has discussed the answers, choose a spokesperson to report your answers to the class.

Language Learning Survey

1. Why are you studying English? How does English study relate to your future goals?

2. How can you improve your listening? What related skills do you need to develop?

3. How can you improve your speaking? What related skills do you need to develop?

4. Have you had previous experience learning in groups? When and where? What does it mean to be a productive group member?

5. How can group learning improve your listening, speaking, reading, and writing skills? What is the difference between group learning and traditional teacher-fronted classrooms?

6. In your previous English classes, what methodology (or method-ologies) did the teacher use? What were some of the advantages and disadvantages of these methodologies?

ACTIVITY 2

In your group, discuss the following questions. Gather as many an-swers as possible from group members. Choose a group spokesperson to report your answers to the class.

Preview Discussion

1. How did you learn to listen, speak, read, and write in your first language and in your second language? Who were your teachers?

2. How did you learn the grammar of your first language? How did you learn the grammar of your second language?

3. What is different about learning your second language?

4. What is language? Write a definition in your group.

ACTIVITY 3

In your groups, try to determine the meanings of the following words. Do not use a dictionary. You will be comparing definitions with those of the other groups, so take notes during your discussion. Choose a spokesperson to present your definitions to the class.

Lecture Vocabulary

1. communicative
2. methodology
3. reinforcement
4. stimulus
5. response
6. specimen
7. phonology
8. morphology
9. acquisition
10. transformational
11. generative
12. syntax/syntactical
13. decontextualized
14. schema
15. semantics
16. affective
17. cognitive
18. lexical

SKILL FOCUS ACTIVITY

ACTIVITY 4

Before the lecture begins, read the following suggestions, and be prepared to answer discussion questions in class.

Notes on Note-Taking

Listening to lectures in a second language is a difficult task. In order to get the important information into your notes, you have to make sense out of the sounds, decide what is important, and write things down on your paper almost simultaneously. Following are some helpful hints.

BEFORE THE LECTURE

1. *Sit in the front.* If you cannot see or hear clearly, you certainly cannot take good notes. Sitting in front also helps you stay attentive and awake. For second-language learners, sitting close to the teacher is essential.

2. *Review your notes.* If you get to the class five minutes early, you can spend five minutes reviewing your notes from the previous class. By doing this, you will already be thinking in English when the class starts. You can also use this time to chat with your group members, compare notes, and review the content vocabulary.

DURING THE LECTURE

1. *Focus your attention on the instructor or the video.* The teacher's body language and facial expressions give you clues as to what he or she thinks is important and help you understand the content better. As you practice with these lectures, imagine the speaker is talking directly to *you*.

2. *Write down everything the teacher writes on the blackboard.* If a teacher takes time to write something on the board, it is important.

3. *Use abbreviations and graphic symbols.* The following symbols can save valuable listening time:

   * or ! = important
   $>$ = greater than
   $<$ = less than
   $\rightarrow$ = results in, leads to
   ?   = I don't understand

   If you need to, invent your own symbols or use your native language to write editorial comments so you do not waste time.

4. *Leave lots of white space.* If your notes are all tightly crammed together, you will not have space to add material when you review your notes later.

AFTER THE LECTURE

1. *Review your notes.* Reviewing your notes immediately after the lecture is absolutely essential. Your memory in a second language is limited unless you are extremely fluent and have experience in academic settings. Native speakers have up to 24 hours before the content of the lecture begins to fade from their memory, and they can no longer easily reconstruct and edit their notes. You, however, may only have a few hours before your notes will begin to fade from your memory. Thus, it is imperative that you review your notes, preferably with another student, as soon as possible after the lecture.

2. *Edit your notes in a different color pen.* There are several reasons for this advice. First, you will be able to see differences between your notes and the notes of your classmates. Because your classmates in this class are second-language learners too, their notes may not always be absolutely correct. Second, you will be able to see where your listening strengths and weaknesses are, and so will your teacher. As you become a better note taker, more and more of your notes will be in one color! Finally, you can write questions and comments in a different color, so you can easily find them later.

3. *Conduct short semiweekly reviews.* If you review your notes merely once, you are going to have a difficult time pulling all of the information together for tests. You should review all of your notes, from beginning to end, *every* few days so you can integrate the ideas, learn the vocabulary, and think about the topic in English.

4. *Write study questions.* In each review session, after you have clarified and edited your notes with your group members, write down questions in another section of your notebook. In this way, you will be preparing for the test. You will learn more about writing study questions later in this unit.

CONTENT ACTIVITY: LECTURE

As you listen to the lectures on language learning, take notes on what you hear. After each of the lectures, review your notes with your group members.

ACTIVITY 5

Lecture Review Outline

Now that you have reviewed all of your notes with your group, you need to go back and look at the lecture as a whole. A good way to do this is to outline the conceptual organization of the lecture. Your outline should show the main points of the lecture in the order in which they were presented.

An outline provides valuable insight into the instructor's teaching goals and probable testing areas. Outlining is helpful for discovering the gist, or essential content, of a lecture or reading. Constructing an outline of the lecture material gives you immediate feedback on how well you understood the main ideas of the lecture and helps you in studying for tests by serving as an organized recall cue. Because it is not necessary to repeat the specific wording of the lecture, outlines are usually written in noun or verb phrases.

The following is a partial outline of the major concepts presented in the lecture. In your groups, use your lecture notes to fill in significant information under each of the major headings. Do not try to include all the details; focus on the information that is necessary to understand and explain the concept. Later you can add more details if you wish. You will be comparing your outline with others. Choose a group spokesperson to share your outline with the class.

I. Introduction

    A. Overview of Lecture

    B. Topic: Second-Language Learning

II. Language Teaching Methodologies/Approaches

    A. Grammar-Translation

    B. ALM

    C. Structuralist Approach

D. Cognitive Approach

E. Content-Based Approach

III. Special Problems of Foreign Students

IV. Conclusion

SKILL FOCUS ACTIVITY

ACTIVITY 6

Writing Study Questions

Writing study questions should become a natural part of your study routine. In college or university courses, most instructors use some kind of evaluation tool to determine what students have learned in the course. The format of the test may be essay, true/false, multiple choice, short answer, or a combination. Your job, then, is to begin preparing for tests from the very first day of class.

Writing study questions has a three-fold purpose. First, you are predicting what the teacher will ask you on a test. Second, when you answer the questions, you are reviewing for the test. You and your study group can use your study questions to prepare for the test. Third, by writing study questions, you learn about the language of testing. Many foreign students find that they fail tests at first not because they did not know the answer but because they did not understand the language, and therefore the meaning, of the questions.

TYPES OF QUESTIONS

A. *True/False*
  True/false questions simply ask the student to decide whether a statement is true or false. Look at the following statement, and decide in your group if it is true or false.

1. _____ The ability to learn language is innate.

You should have decided that this statement is false because the proposition presented is a hypothesis, which, by definition, is neither true nor false. Consider the following:

2. _____ Chomsky argues that the ability to learn language is innate.

Now the proposition is true, based on the information given in the lecture. When you answer true/false items, keep in mind that if *any part* of the proposition is false, the entire item is false.

B. *Multiple Choice*
  Multiple choice test items ask the student to choose the best or most appropriate response from a list of four or five possible answers. The following is a typical multiple choice item:

1. Classroom activities developed for use in the audiolingual method include
   a. pattern practice, repetition drills, and grammar-translation.
   b. repetition drills, grammar-translation, and error correction.
   c. repetition drills, pattern practice, and substitution drills.
   d. error correction, pattern practice, and grammar-translation.

The correct answer is *c*. As noted in the lecture, grammar-translation is used in the classical or grammar-translation method.

Practice: In your groups, write five true/false and five multiple choice test items. Your teacher will collect them and help you revise them if needed.

C. *Short Answer*
  Short answer questions often ask students to define terms or concepts, as they relate to the topic of study. Answers to these questions

should be no longer than a paragraph and should include examples where necessary to clearly explain the term. Following is an example of this kind of question.

1. Identify grammar-translation.

A good answer, given the information in the lecture, would be, "The grammar-translation, or classical, method refers to an older method of teaching a second language, which emphasizes reading and writing, with little or no emphasis on speaking. Instruction in this method uses the mother tongue, and class time is spent reading and translating literature. Grammar-translation is used to teach Latin and Greek. Students who learn their second language through this method may not be able to understand, speak, or write the language well."

Practice: In your groups, write five short answer questions, which require definitions of terms or concepts from the lecture.

D. Essay Questions
In your groups, try to define the following terms. Do not use a dictionary.

1. describe
2. summarize
3. state
4. analyze
5. compare
6. contrast
7. discuss
8. evaluate
9. interpret
10. support
11. prove
12. trace
13. enumerate
14. criticize

Any of the preceding words may be used in essay questions. An essay question asks students to demonstrate their mastery of the course readings and lectures. Essay questions are usually new questions, that is, questions that the instructor and the students have not previously discussed. These questions may require the student to integrate reading and lecture material to create the answer. Generally, essay questions require students to write a page or two. These essays should be well organized; they should have an introduction with a thesis or controlling idea that answers the question; they should have a body; and they should have a conclusion. Important ideas should be supported with examples. The instructor is usually looking for how much of the content material the student knows, how the student uses that knowledge to solve problems, and how well the student supports his or her own ideas. Often essay questions consist of several parts. Following are examples of essay questions:

A. Describe content-based language teaching.

B. Compare and contrast the audiolingual method with the grammar-translation approach.

Practice: In your groups, write five essay questions related to the language learning lecture. Use the terms listed previously.

CONTENT ACTIVITIES: READING

A C T I V I T Y 7

Answer the following questions *before* beginning to read "Memory for Prose."

Reading Preview Questions

1. What is the main idea of this reading? (Check the title and subtitles, look for illustrations, and read the first and last paragraphs to find main ideas.)

2. What do you already know about this topic? Make a quick list of ideas or words that come to mind.

3. Read the questions that follow the reading, and look for the answers as you read.

Now read the following passage.

Memory for Prose

Memory plays an integral part in listening from the moment the first sound hits our ears to our recollection, years later, of what was said. In the construction process it is the halfway house where sounds and words are stored, and it is the final storehouse for the propositions that are built from them. In the utilization process it is the place where new information is stored, asked-for information is sought, and planned actions are placed. It is also the archive for the facts and general knowledge that are used in inferring indirect meanings. This chapter focuses on one aspect of this capacity: memory for passages once heard or read....

WHAT AFFECTS MEMORY?

Memory for prose depends on many factors:

1. *Type of language.* Was the passage an ordinary conversation, a formal lecture, a play, a poem, or a list of unrelated sentences in a psychology experiment?
2. *Input.* Did we hear it passively, try to memorize it word for word, listen for the gist only, or listen for nothing but grammatical errors?
3. *Retention interval.* Did we hear it a moment ago or a year ago?
4. *Output.* Are we trying to recall it verbatim, or only trying to decide for a test sentence whether or not it was what we had originally heard?

Source: "What Affects Memory?" from "Memory for Prose" in *Psychology and Language* by Herbert H. Clark and Eve E. Clark, copyright © 1977 by Harcourt Brace Jovanovich, Inc., reprinted by permission of the publisher.

All of these factors affect the content and accuracy of what we remember.

To say "I remember x" is to make one of three claims. For example, the statement "I remember that Ken told Julia 'Come here'" is a claim that Ken uttered the exact words **Come here**. However, "I remember that Ken told Julia to come here" is a claim, not about Ken's exact words, but about the intended interpretation or "gist" of his message. Again, "I remember Lincoln's *Gettysburg Address*" is a claim about one's ability to repeat the speech word for word. It is not a claim about an event that took place at the time something came into memory, but about an enduring piece of general knowledge. These distinctions between verbatim and gist memory, and between episodic and general memory, are each important to the remembering process.

But what is most important about this characterization is that remembering is *making claims about* past events, not merely "retrieving" representations of the events themselves. While remembering does require that information be retrieved from memory, like notes fetched from a pigeonhole, these notes are used only as a starting point for the claims. The notes will usually be incomplete, garbled, and even contrary to common sense. But since people can safely assume that the original passage did not contain these flaws, they will not want to claim that it did. They will make corrections to insure that their claim sounds sensible. For reasons like this, remembering is often said to be a reconstructive process. People remember passages by piecing together what information they can retrieve, adding outside information and making corrections wherever necessary to get them to make sense.

In its barest outlines, remembering has three stages: input, storage, and output. The pigeonhole analogy will serve nicely here. On hearing a passage, listeners jot down notes about its contents on pieces of paper. This is the input. Next, they place these notes in a pigeonhole in memory until they need them. This is storage. During this time some of the notes can become lost or smudged. At the time of recall, they fetch the notes from their pigeonhole and from this fragmentary information reconstruct what they thought was in the original message. This is the output. It is instructive to examine these three stages more closely before turning to memory more generally.

Input
Normally, in conversation, people take in speech, build interpretations, purge memory of the exact wording, and go on to use their interpretations for their intended purposes. People generally listen for meaning. They do not store the verbatim wording or even the direct meaning of the speech, which is used only for drawing further inferences. Instead, they normally store the inferences themselves, the

situation modeled, or whatever else the interpretations have been used for. It should come as no surprise, then, that people cannot usually recall speech word for word. They were listening not for what was said but for what was meant.

In "unusual" situations, however, verbatim memory can become important. An actor may have to memorize *Hamlet*, a student Keats's "Ode on a Grecian Urn," and a churchgoer the Lord's Prayer. When they do this, they apply a rather special skill, one that requires repetition and much hard work. The same people would be utterly unable to listen to a conversation and reproduce it word for word an hour later. So memorization, though clearly a topic of memory, is unrepresentative of the "normal" course of input and may require very different processes.

The input situations that have actually been studied run the gamut from the "normal" to the "unusual" — from listening for meaning to outright memorization. Most fall nearer the "unusual" end of the continuum. For example, when people are asked to read ten unrelated sentences and then recall them, they do not read for meaning alone. They try to memorize, to pay close attention to the surface details, for they want to be able to recall the sentences word for word. So what do these experiments tell us about the "normal" situations? Recent experiments suggest that "normal" situations are quite different. The input situation is one of the most critical determinants of what people remember.

Storage

Psychologists have traditionally distinguished between short-term memory and long-term memory (but see Craik and Lockhart, 1972). *Short-term memory* is a place where exact wording is stored for brief periods of time. Words can be maintained there only through active rehearsal — as when we repeat telephone numbers to ourselves — and are otherwise lost very rapidly. Short-term memory has a limited capacity. It can hold only about seven or so unrelated words at a time. *Long-term memory*, on the other hand, is the place where more permanent information is stored. It deals generally in meaning rather than sounds, and for all practical purposes it has unlimited capacity. The information in long-term memory is often divided theoretically into episodic information (facts about everyday events that can be dated) and general knowledge (facts and generalizations that cannot be dated) (Tulving, 1972). Although this chapter will continually refer to general knowledge, it is primarily concerned with memory for episodic information.

In the traditional framework, short-term memory corresponds roughly to what has been called the working memory in the construction process. You will recall that working memory is where the phonological content and isolated constituents of a sentence are placed. Just like short-term memory, it stores surface features, can handle only a limited capacity, and loses its contents very rapidly. But working memory is also the place where the interpretation of a sentence is first stored. Unfortunately, very little is known about the storage of interpretations in short-term memory, so it is hard to see whether it corresponds to working memory in this way or not (but see Craik and Lockhart, 1972; Shulman, 1970, 1972). Working memory, then, may differ slightly from traditional views of short-term memory.

Long-term memory for episodes is most often claimed to be in the form of a network of propositions, perhaps accompanied by visual, auditory, and other kinds of imagery (see Chase and H. Clark, 1972; Kintsch, 1972, 1974; Rumelhart, Lindsay, and Norman, 1972). This view has been implicit so far in the construction and utilization processes. The interpretations of a sentence consist of propositions, and in the utilization process, they were added to memory, retrieved from memory, and compared against other propositions in memory. The role of imagery in memory for prose is much less clear and will be touched on only peripherally.

In the memorization of prose, however, long-term memory must also be able to store verbatim forms accompanied perhaps by such auxiliary information as "the first word was **four-score**," "the sentence was in the active voice," and "there were many multisyllabic words." The verbatim content may not even be accompanied by meaning in the usual sense. Some Hausa-speaking Nigerians, for example, memorize the whole Koran without knowing a word of classical Arabic, the language of the Koran. So long-term memory must have the capacity to store verbatim forms alone.

Output
The two methods for tapping memory are recognition and recall. In a recognition test, people are shown a sentence and asked if it was one they had seen or heard before. They may be shown two or more sentences and asked to point to the one they had seen or heard before. In a recall test, on the other hand, people have to produce or write down a sentence or passage they had been given previously. Sometimes they are prompted with a word or phrase — like the subject of a sentence — and asked to recall the corresponding sentence. Recognition is usually more accurate than recall.

In both recognition and recall, people utilize three kinds of outside information. They may refer to their language to decide what are possible, sensible constructions, and what are not. They may use world knowledge to decide what are plausible realistic situations or events, and what are not. (This is the reality principle.) And finally, they may refer to conventions about discourse to decide how stories are constructed, how paragraphs are organized, and how conversations proceed. Such information makes it possible to rule out sentences that could not have occurred and settle on ones that could. Linguistic knowledge, world knowledge, and conventions of discourse have striking consequences for the recognition and recall of prose.

The rest of this chapter takes up the input, storage, and output processes pertinent to memory for prose. It begins with verbatim recall, works through memory for more and more abstract features of the language input, and concludes with memory for paragraphs, stories, and other kinds of discourse This progression follows the characteristics of the input—what people were listening for, and what kind of passage they were listening to. Memory adheres to the dictum: You can't get out what you haven't put in.

ACTIVITY ⑧

Reading Questions

1. What are the three stages of remembering?

2. Why are people usually not able to recall speech word for word?

3. What is the difference between short-term and long-term memory?

4. What are two methods for tapping memory, and how are they different?

A C T I V I T Y 9

In your groups, discuss the following questions. Use your answers from the reading questions to help you answer them. Choose a spokesperson to report your answers to the class.

Reading Discussion Questions

1. According to the textbook passage, the input situation is one of the critical determinants of *what* people remember. What do you think are some of the differences between experimental situations and "normal" situations?

2. How does the example of the Hausa-speaking Nigerians who memorize the Koran relate to short- and long-term memory? What are some possible methods the Nigerians might use to help them store and retrieve the content of the Koran?

3. Why do you think recognition is easier than recall? How might this aspect of memory function apply to the skills of listening, speaking, reading, and writing? How might it apply to taking academic tests?

4. Many students of English as a second or foreign language need to take the TOEFL test, which is divided into three or four sections. In the first section, students usually listen to a dialogue and then answer questions about the dialogue. What aspects of memory are involved in taking this section of the test? Can you think of any strategies that students might use to help them do well in this section of the test?

PROBLEM-SOLVING ACTIVITIES

ACTIVITY 10

Language Experiment

After your teacher conducts the experiment, answer the following questions in your groups. Take notes on your answers. You will be reporting your answers to the rest of the class.

1. How many words did each group member remember? The group secretary should write the totals on a piece of paper.

2. Why did some students remember more words than other students did? Interview the students with super memories, and try to find out if they used any particular recall strategies.

3. After interviewing the subjects of the experiment, consider the process of the experiment. How was the experiment conducted? What materials were used? Was each subject given the same task?

4. What did the experiment demonstrate? What can the results tell us about the nature or process of human memory? How do the results relate to schema theory?

A C T I V I T Y 11

Follow-Up Experiment

You can test other students in your school to see if the experiment brings similar results. You need two sets of cards; each card has 25 words typed or printed neatly on it. All of the cards must have the same 25 words on them. Set A cards present the words arranged categorically, whereas set B cards mix the words randomly. If you test second-language learners, choose categories of words that are easily recognizable because the students only have one minute to study the cards. As you plan the experiment with your group, consider the language ability of the students you will test. You must also consider how you will conduct the test and how you will tabulate the results.

Here is a plan to help you organize the experiment.

1. Choose subjects for study.
2. Decide on five categories of words to include.
3. Select five recognizable words from each category.
4. Write the words, arranged categorically, on set A cards.
5. Write the words, arranged randomly, on set B cards.
6. Choose a time and place to conduct the experiment.
7. Tabulate the results.
8. Report the results to the class.

EVALUATION ACTIVITIES

A C T I V I T Y 12

Test Review

Your teacher will distribute the study questions that your class wrote for this unit. In your groups, review your notes to make sure you have the information to answer the questions.

ACTIVITY 13

Test Correction

In your groups, review your answers to the test questions. If an answer is wrong, try to determine why and then try to find the correct answer. If you cannot determine why an answer is wrong, ask your teacher for assistance.

ACTIVITY 14

Scenarios

Each group will receive one copy of a scenario role, and your group will have 10 to 15 minutes to prepare for this activity.

ACTIVITY 15

After your class has rehearsed, performed, and discussed the scenarios, complete the following exercise.

Student Scenario Worksheet

1. *Vocabulary and idioms.* Write as many of the new words as you can remember from today's scenarios.

2. *Topic and roles.* What was the topic of each scenario? Write a brief description of the different roles performed by the students; include a description of the performers' goals.

3. *Strategies.* How did the student performers try to accomplish their goals? What particular strategies were most effective? Who had the most control during the conversations? Why?

4. *Structures.* Write examples of new constructions learned today. What grammar points are illustrated?

ACTIVITY 16

Answer the following questions concerning your experience working in your group. Be as explicit as you can. Only your teacher will read your answers, but you will be asked if you would like to share some of your answers in a class discussion.

Feedback Questionnaire

1. What kind of communication problems did your group encounter during the unit? How did you solve the problems?

2. Were all of your group members in class every day? What happened to the group if someone was absent? What happened to the absentee group member when he or she came back?

3. Did your group usually stay on task? If not, what happened?

4. Did your group have a leader? What was the effect on the group of having a leader or of not having a leader?

5. What problems did your group encounter that may have been related to cultural differences? How did you solve the problems?

6. What did you learn about group dynamics from working in your group? What did you learn about yourself?

7. How did you contribute to the success or failure of your group?

8. What were some of the advantages of working in your group? What were some of the disadvantages?

9. What plans do you have to change your behavior in your next group? How will this change help you learn English better?

10. What suggestions do you have to give your teacher concerning the activities that your group completed in this unit?

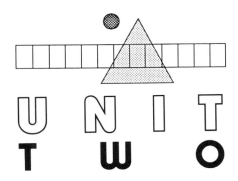

UNIT
TWO

Demography

PREVIEW ACTIVITIES

Your teacher will divide your class into groups. These groups will remain the same throughout this unit.

ACTIVITY 1

In your groups, discuss the following questions. Gather as many answers as possible from group members. Choose a spokesperson to report your answers to the class.

Preview Discussion

1. What is the population of your country? Is it growing? Is it declining? Which parts (age, sex, economic, racial, or national groups) are growing? Which parts are declining? What reasons can you give for their growth or decline?

2. What are the migration patterns in your country? Why do people move from one area of your country to another? How does this movement affect the place the people leave and the place to which they move? Why do people leave your country, and/or why do people move to your country? What is the effect of this migration on your country's economy and society?

3. The world population is predicted to double in 35 years. In which geographic areas do you think most of this growth will occur? What kinds of global problems do you think will result from this increase in population?

ACTIVITY 2

In your groups, try to determine the meanings of the following words. Do not use a dictionary. You will be comparing your definitions with those of the other groups, so take notes during your discussion. Choose a spokesperson to report your definitions to the class.

Lecture Vocabulary

1. equation
2. net (n)
3. estimate (v)
4. calculate
5. crude
6. ratio
7. index
8. accumulation
9. reallocate
10. investment
11. implement (v)
12. variable
13. times (v)
14. prenatal
15. plus
16. minus

$$P_{t+n} = P_t + B_n - D_n + IM_n - OM_n$$

FIGURE 2.1   The demographic equation

$$CBR = \frac{Births}{Midyear\ population} \times 1,000$$

FIGURE 2.2   Crude birth rate

$$\text{CDR} = \frac{\text{Deaths}}{\text{Midyear population}} \times 1,000$$

FIGURE 2.3 Crude death rate

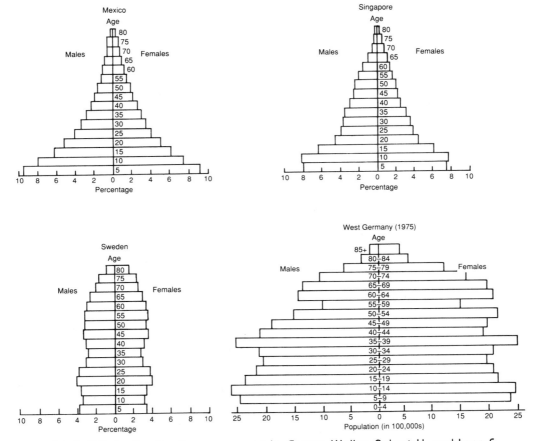

FIGURE 2.4 Age-sex pyramids. *Source:* Weller, Robert H. and Leon F. Bouvier, *Population: Demography and Policy* (New York: St. Martin's Press), 1981, pp. 243–245. Reprinted by permission of the authors.

CONTENT ACTIVITY: LECTURE

As you listen to the lectures on demography, take notes on what you hear. After each of the lectures, review your notes with your group members. After you have reviewed the notes, write the study questions that your teacher assigns.

ACTIVITY 3

Now that you have reviewed all your notes in your group, outline the main ideas of the lecture in the space provided. Focus on the organization of the lecture, rather than on details. Choose a spokesperson to share your outline with the class.

Lecture Review Outline

I. Introduction

   A. Definition of Demography

   B. Areas of Investigation for Demographers

   C. Demographic Variables

II. Demographic Equation

III. Measuring World Population Growth

IV. Sex and Age Composition

V. Policies Based on Demographic Data

SKILL FOCUS ACTIVITY

ACTIVITY 4

Describing a Problem-Solving Process

As a student, you will be required to solve problems, that is, to apply information (formulas or equations, approaches, data) to new situations. You may have to provide a solution and describe the processes, the steps, you followed to reach the solution. Following are four demographic problems. In your groups, solve the problems and be prepared to explain to the class the steps you followed to arrive at your solutions. Choose a spokesperson to report your results to the class.

HELPFUL VOCABULARY

First (second, third) _____. Then (next) we _____.

Using a rate of _____, we can calculate _____.

Looking at the _____, we see that _____.

By (dividing, multiplying) _____ by _____, we get _____.

If we add _____ to _____, we get _____.

Subtract _____ from _____. The result is _____.

Round off to the nearest _____.

The ratio of _____ to _____ is _____.

The percentage increase (decrease) is _____.

Problem 1. Population for area B in 1985 was 1,273,916. Using the demographic equation (see Figure 2.1), find the population for 1986 based on the information given in Table 2.1.

T A B L E 2 . 1 Population in 1986

YEAR	1986
POPULATION	_____
BIRTHS	20,486
DEATHS	16,013
IN-MIGRATION	17,372
OUT-MIGRATION	11,966

Problem 2. Using Table 2.2, compute sex ratios for each age cohort. Round off to the nearest tenth.

Problem 3. Using Table 2.2, calculate the index of aging for both sexes and for the total population. Round off to the nearest tenth.

T A B L E   2 . 2 Age Cohorts

AGE COHORT	MALES	FEMALES	SEX RATIO
0–4	6,684*	6,104	109.5
5–9	6,470	5,941	108.9
10–14	9,503	8,743	108.6
15–19	9,621	8,966	103.3
20–24	7,755	8,843	87.7
25–29	7,487	8,706	86.0
30–34	6,496	8,593	———
35–39	5,427	7,334	———
40–44	4,646	6,279	———
45–49	3,755	5,145	———
50–54	3,904	4,067	———
55–59	3,596	3,826	———
60–65	3,380	3,611	———
66–69	1,597	2,576	———
70–74	1,072	1,891	———
75–79	506	1,034	———
80–84	405	906	———
85 +	298	805	———
TOTAL	———	———	———

INDEX OF AGING		
	Males	———
	Females	———
	Total Population	———

*in thousands

Problem 4. Table 2.3 gives the number of live births, the number of deaths, the female population aged 15–49, and the total population for country X and country Y. Calculate the crude birth rate (see Figure 2.2), the crude death rate (see Figure 2.3), the crude growth rate, and the fertility rate for each country. Round off to the nearest tenth.

TABLE 2.3 Births and Female Population

COUNTRY	X	Y
BIRTHS	1,476,842	1,446,302
DEATHS	1,347,791	1,176,817
FEMALES (15–49)	30,404,641	22,396,283
POPULATION	128,672,971	129,865,186

COUNTRY	CBR	CDR	CRUDE GROWTH RATE	GENERAL FERTILITY RATE
X	_____	_____	_____	_____
Y	_____	_____	_____	_____

CONTENT ACTIVITIES: READING

ACTIVITY 5

Answer the following questions *before* beginning to read "The Elderly and Social Security."

Reading Preview Questions

1. What is the main idea of this reading? (Check the title and subtitles, look for illustrations, read the first and last paragraphs to find main ideas.)

2. What do you already know about this topic? Make a quick list of ideas or words that come to mind.

3. Read the questions that follow the reading, and look for the answers as you read.

Now read the following passage.

The Elderly and Social Security

In 1940 there were 9 million elderly people (age sixty-five and over) in the United States.[1] By 1980 the number had almost tripled to about 25 million. It will undoubtedly surpass 30 million at the turn of the century and reach 52 million by 2030. The elderly population has grown much faster than has the total population. During this century the number of persons sixty-five and over will have increased tenfold, whereas the nation's total population will have increased only fourfold. The larger than average gains in the number of older people are the result of the high fertility of sixty-five and seventy-five years ago and lower fertility since then. [Figure 2.5] shows the percent increase in the number of elderly for each decade since 1900. The birth cohorts of the last portion of the nineteenth century and the first decades of this century were quite large. Although mortality was high (relative to current levels), these cohorts were still large when they attained age sixty-five.

Fertility dropped sharply during the 1920s and 1930s. The effects of this decline will appear in 1990 when the rate of growth of the elderly population will drop to well under 10 percent. Fertility increased sharply during the baby boom. These cohorts will begin reaching age sixty-five about the year 2010. During that decade the elderly population will increase sharply—perhaps by as much as 30 percent. Because of the baby bust of the 1970s the size of the elderly population will actually be reduced between 2030 and 2040. . . .

The potential problems associated with the future growth of the aged population naturally lead to a discussion of the social security system. The federally operated system is funded by deductions from the wages of workers and employers; these monies are distributed to beneficiaries of a specified age, sometimes age sixty-two and most often sixty-five. If the number of workers equals the number of beneficiaries, there are no major problems. When the number of workers exceeds the beneficiaries (as will occur in the 1990s), a surplus of funds develops. And when the beneficiaries outnumber the workers who contribute to the system, a deficit emerges.

Currently social security is experiencing financial problems, in

[1]The terms "elderly," "aged," and "older people" will be used interchangeably in this section. While recent tendencies have been to elevate the age of retirement to seventy, we are following the conventional practice of using age sixty-five as the breaking point, in line with social security regulations.

Source: Weller, Robert H. and Leon F. Bouvier, *Population: Demography and Policy* (New York: St. Martin's Press), 1981, pp. 264–270. Reprinted by permission of the authors.

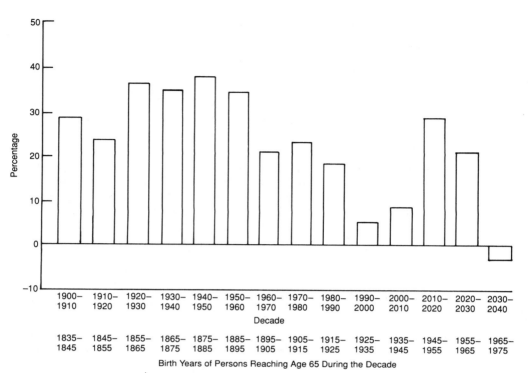

F I G U R E 2 . 5 Decennial percent change of the population sixty-five years and older, 1900–2040 (*Source:* U.S. Bureau of the Census, 1976.)

part because of the increasing elderly population. (A number of other nondemographic issues are also involved but do not concern us here.) These problems are expected to increase around 2010, when the baby boom generation begins swelling the elderly population. The middle-aged persons who will be working during that decade and paying into the social security pool will be those of the smaller baby bust generation. Thus, fewer economically active people will be paying for the "welfare" of an increased number of elderly. Because of this potential problem, some economists have argued for an increase in fertility to provide for a larger labor force in the next century. But most people agree that this "solution" would create more problems than it would solve. . . .

Looking only at the elderly population overstates the argument for increased fertility and greatly oversimplifies the issue of dependency. As [Figure 2.6] shows, the massive growth in the elderly population in the early part of the next century does translate into a rapidly falling ratio of taxpayers (covered workers) to beneficiaries: from five in 1960 to just over two per beneficiary by 2030. But if fertility remains low, the proportion of children will decrease as will

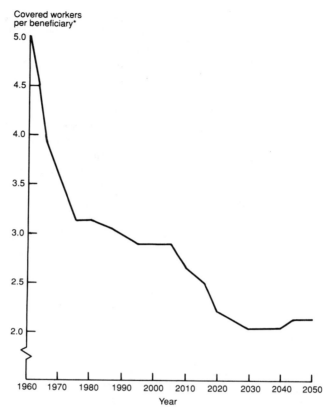

Covered workers
per beneficiary*

*Based on Alternative II of 1978 *Trustee's Report:*
total fertility rate = 2.1, unemployment rate = 5.0.

F I G U R E   2 . 6   Number of covered workers per beneficiary of old-age, survivors', and disability insurance programs, 1960–2050 (*Source:* Select Committee on Population, 1978, p. 73.)

expenditures for their welfare. This will compensate for the increase in the elderly population. Rather than concentrate solely on the future proportion age sixty-five or older, economic planners should be looking at the total dependency ratio. Doing so yields a more complete picture.

. . . We defined the dependent years as fourteen or younger and sixty-five or older. In countries such as the United States, seventeen is a more realistic cutoff age for the young dependents. Because the necessary data are available, we have used age seventeen as the upper limit of the younger dependent age group and sixty-five as the lower limit of older dependents, with those eighteen to sixty-four representing the economically active age groups.

In 1980 there were 62.0 dependents per 100 active persons. If fertility continues at its present low level, by 2000 the dependency ratio will have *dropped* to 53.7. Even in 2020 (when members of the baby boom cohort begin to retire) the total dependency ratio will be only 57.9 per 100. Thus the total dependency load will not increase if fertility remains low. Instead, the number (and percent) of young dependents will decrease. Although the growing elderly population will present problems to society, a major problem after 2020 may well be that of developing the will and commitment necessary to balance our expenditures for the young with those for the aged.

Shifting the emphasis from one age group to another age group is far from simple. In economic, social, and political terms, the two age groups are by no means equivalent. Still the decreased consumption of the young will considerably offset the increased consumption of the old. In 1976 health expenditures (public and private) totaled $120 billion. Of this, approximately $19 billion was spent on behalf of those under twenty and $35 billion by and for those sixty-five and over. . . . Total expenditures in 1976 for education were also $120 billion, of which about $90 billion was for the under-twenty age group. . . . According to economist Alan Sweezy, the total drain on the national product for those two items of consumption was $109 billion by the young and $35 billion for the aged. If, in 1976, we had had the age distribution projected for 2030–2050, these figures would have been $86 and $57 billion, respectively. Thus, the young would have consumed $23 billion less and the elderly $22 billion more of health and educational services.

ACTIVITY 6

Using information from the reading, answer the following questions.

Reading Questions

1. What is the demographic change described and analyzed in the article?

2. How does the U.S. social security system work?

3. What problems do the authors foresee in this demographic change? What solution do the authors propose to the funding problem of an aging population?

4. How do the authors support their solution?

ACTIVITY 7

In your groups, discuss the following questions. Use your answers from the reading questions to help you answer them. Choose a spokesperson to report your answers to the class.

Reading Discussion Questions

1. Using demographic data, the authors of the article "The Elderly and Social Security" and the lecturer predicted that the aging of the populations of industrialized nations would create problems. How do their solutions to the problems differ?

2. The lecturer suggests that economic and social problems would accompany the importation of workers from the less developed countries to the industrialized countries. What would some of the economic and social problems be? Specify the problems for both the countries the workers left and the countries they entered.

3. What other solutions could you design for the aging population problems in developed countries?

SKILL FOCUS ACTIVITY

ACTIVITY 8

Predicting/Inferencing

In the lecture, the speaker said that demographic data have been used to predict future economic and social problems. These predictions are then used to develop policies to deal with the problems. The speaker mentioned the efforts by the Chinese government to control population growth. The speaker also mentioned the article by Jonathan Rauch, who suggested that industrial nations import workers from developing nations to support aging populations in the industrial world. In both examples, demographic information provided the initial data, from which predictions about future problems, economic and social, were made. In China it was predicted that enormous population growth would prevent resources from being used to develop the country economically. Rauch said that the aging of populations in industrialized countries could not be supported in terms of social security and medical care by a significantly decreased workforce.

As a student, you will be required to make predictions or inferences (conclusions) from data. In order to make effective predictions, you must examine the data for *all probable effects*, that is, all effects or consequences that can be reasonably predicted from the data. In addition, you must include enough facts to support your conclusions or predictions.

In your groups, look again at the results of your calculations for problems 2 through 4 in Activity 4 on page 29. What predictions can you make with these data? Begin with statements about the data itself. What do the data show? What trends can you see in the data? What might happen in the next few years? Try to predict reasonable economic and social consequences of the data. Support your predictions. Gather as many predictions as you can in your groups. Choose a spokesperson to report your predictions to the class.

HELPFUL VOCABULARY

The data show _____.

We can expect (predict) _____ because (since) _____.

Therefore (consequently, so) _____.

It follows that _____.

The data point to _____.

The effect of _____ might (may) be to _____.

_____ might cause (lead to) _____.

Assuming that _____, _____.

The reason for _____ is _____.

If we project these figures, then _____.

PROBLEM-SOLVING ACTIVITY

A C T I V I T Y 9

Product Marketing

Imagine you are a marketing manager in a company that wants to develop and market new products in cities A, B, and C. (Refer to Figures 2.7, 2.8, and 2.9.) Discuss the demographic data. Then decide what products you think you could develop and market well in each of the areas. Be prepared to explain your products, to discuss why you think they would sell well in the area, and to describe how you plan to market them. Choose a spokesperson to describe your group's products, your reasons for choosing these products, and your marketing strategy.

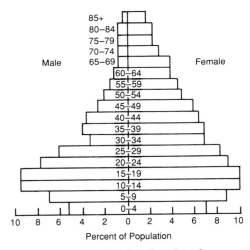

F I G U R E 2 . 7 City A

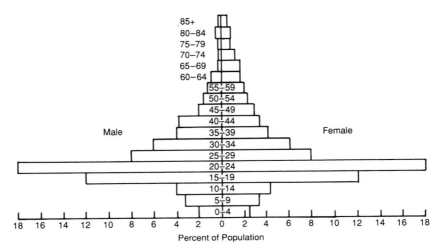

F I G U R E   2 . 8   City B

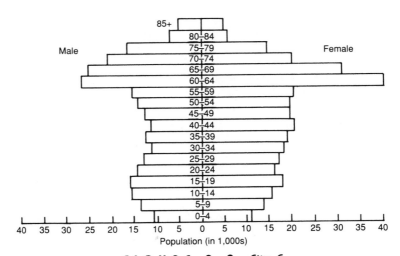

F I G U R E   2 . 9   City C

EVALUATION ACTIVITIES

ACTIVITY 10

Test Review

Your teacher will distribute the study questions that your class wrote for this unit. In your groups, review your notes to make sure you have the information to answer the questions.

ACTIVITY 11

Test Correction

In your groups, review your answers to the test questions. If an answer is wrong, try to determine why, and then try to find the correct answer. If you cannot determine why an answer is wrong, ask your teacher for assistance.

ACTIVITY 12

Answer the following questions concerning your experience working in your group. Be as explicit as you can. Only your teacher will read your answers, but you will be asked if you would like to share some of your answers in a class discussion.

Feedback Questionnaire

1. What kind of communication problems did your group encounter during the unit? How did you solve the problems?

2. Were all of your group members in class every day? What happened to the group if someone was absent? What happened to the absentee group member when he or she came back?

3. Did your group usually stay on task? If not, what happened?

4. Did your group have a leader? What was the effect on the group of having a leader or of not having a leader?

5. What problems did your group encounter that may have been related to cultural differences? How did you solve the problems?

6. What did you learn about group dynamics from working in your group? What did you learn about yourself?

7. How did you contribute to the success or failure of your group?

8. What were some of the advantages of working in your group? What were some of the disadvantages?

9. What plans do you have to change your behavior in your next group? How will this change help you learn English better?

10. What suggestions do you have to give to your teacher concerning the activities that your group completed in this unit?

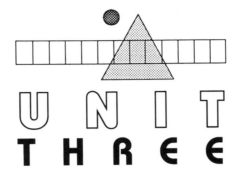

UNIT
THREE

The American Civil Rights Movement 1954–59

PREVIEW ACTIVITIES

Your teacher will divide your class into groups. These groups will remain the same throughout this unit.

A C T I V I T Y 1

In your group, discuss the following questions. Gather as many answers as possible from each group member. Choose a group spokesperson to report your ideas to the class.

Preview Discussion

1. When did slavery begin and end in the United States? Why was it begun? How did it end?

2. What is racism and how does it affect society?

3. What are your civil rights? Are they the same for all humans? Why or why not?

4. What is civil disobedience?

5. Who were the leaders of the civil rights movement in the United States? For what were they fighting?

6. When did black Americans receive fair and equal treatment under the law?

ACTIVITY 2

In your groups, try to determine the meanings of the following words. Do not use a dictionary. You will be comparing your definitions with those of the other groups, so take notes during your discussion. Choose a spokesperson to report your definitions to the class.

Lecture Vocabulary

1. representatives	7. tyranny	13. injustice
2. abolitionist	8. landmark decision	14. casket
3. discrimination	9. inherent	15. tacit
4. integration	10. safeguard	16. testimony
5. doctrine	11. potent	17. coalition
6. segregation	12. electorate	18. foes

ACTIVITY 3

Identifying Key People, Events, and Issues

During the lecture, listen for information about the following names or terms. At the conclusion of each segment of the lecture, verify your information with your group members. Choose a spokesperson to report your answers to the class.

1. Jim Crow Laws
2. Emmett Till
3. Mose Wright

4. Rosa Parks
5. The Reverend Martin Luther King, Jr.
6. The Little Rock Nine
7. Civil Rights Act of 1964
8. Voting Rights Act
9. *Plessy* v. *Ferguson* Decision
10. *Brown* v. *Board of Education* Decision

CONTENT ACTIVITY: LECTURE

As you listen to the lectures on the early years of the American civil rights movement, take notes on what you hear. After each of the lectures, review your notes with your group members. After you have reviewed the notes, write the study questions that your teacher assigns.

A C T I V I T Y 4

Now that you have reviewed all your notes in your group, outline the main ideas of the lecture in the space provided. Focus on the organization of the lecture rather than on details. Choose a spokesperson to share your outline with the class.

Lecture Review Outline

I. History of Slavery

II. Segregation and Integration: 1896–1954
    A. *Plessy* v. *Ferguson*

III. Early Civil Rights Movement
   A. Emmett Till Case

IV. Achievements of Movement

V. Conclusion

SKILL FOCUS ACTIVITY

ACTIVITY 5

Displaying, Interpreting, and Reporting Data on Graphs

As a college or university student, you will be required to understand graphs in textbooks, magazines, or journals. Graphs allow the reader to visualize the information and to see relationships, which the author wishes to emphasize, among the data. Graphs can take various forms. The form of a graph will be determined by the data and the purpose of the author. The horizontal axis of a graph shows the independent variable that is being used to study the effects of the dependent variable on the vertical axis. Time or distance are common independent variables.

In order to see the effect of the scale of a graph, look at the graphs illustrated in Figures 3.1 and 3.2. Now consider that a beach resort in the Caribbean is preparing an advertisement for newspapers and magazines. The resort wants to attract more vacationers. Which graph would be more suitable for the ad?

Both graphs contain the same information, but the scale of the two axes makes a big difference in the impression created by the graph. As you can see, the proportions of the graph in Figure 3.2 give a better impression of the stability of the temperature, which would attract more tourists.

In the following problems, your group will construct graphs and then choose a spokesperson to explain them to the class.

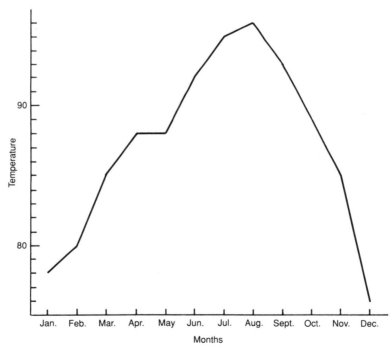

F I G U R E   3 . 1   Average monthly temperatures in the Caribbean

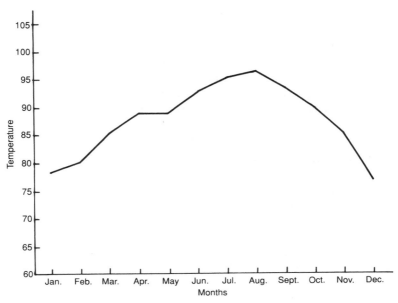

F I G U R E   3 . 2   Average monthly temperatures in the Caribbean

Problems*

1. Create a time line to illustrate the significant historical, political, and social events that were defined in the lecture. What will this time line represent? Write a descriptive title for the visual presentation, and be prepared to explain it to the rest of the class.

2. Using the following data, construct a graph that illustrates the change in poverty rates for blacks and whites in 25 years. Make the portions representative and easy to read. Title the graph.

    In 1959, 56.2 percent of blacks were living in poverty. That figure decreased to 30.3 percent by 1974, but it increased to 33.8 percent in 1984. In 1959, 18.1 percent of whites lived in poverty. This figure decreased to 8.4 percent by 1974, and it was 11.5 percent in 1984. After you construct your graph, discuss with your group members the possible reasons for the increase in poverty rates from 1974 to 1984.

*Data in these problems are from the U.S. Departments of Commerce, Education, Labor, and Health and Human Services, 1986.

3. Using the following data, construct a graph that illustrates the change in educational patterns from 1964 to 1984. Make your percentages representative and easy to read. Title the graph.

   In 1964, 7 percent of blacks and 21 percent of whites aged 18–24 were in college. In 1984, 19 percent of blacks and 27 percent of whites aged 18–24 were in college.

4. Using the following data, construct a graph that illustrates the changing status of unemployed black males. Title the graph.

   In 1970, 433,000 black males were unemployed. That figure has continued to rise: 916,000 in 1975, 1,034,000 in 1980, and 1,103,000 in 1985. Can you think of any reasons this figure is rising?

5. Using the following data, construct two pie charts that illustrate the changing careers of black workers. Title the graph.

   In 1965, 19.5 percent of employed blacks held white collar jobs; 41 percent held blue collar jobs; 1.6 percent were household help; 7.8 percent worked on farms; and 19.1 percent performed some other service. In 1985, 40.9 percent of employed blacks held white collar jobs; 32.5 percent held blue collar jobs; 2.8 percent were household help; 2.6 percent worked on farms; and 21.2 percent performed some other service. To what can we attribute these changes?

HELPFUL VOCABULARY

The following vocabulary is often used when describing graphs.

The graph shows _____.

The graph illustrates _____.

The horizontal axis represents _____.

The vertical axis represents _____.

This figure decreased (increased) in (year) to _____.

CONTENT ACTIVITIES: READING

ACTIVITY 6

Answer the following questions *before* beginning to read "Activism: Women, Chicanos, Indians."

Reading Preview Questions

1. What is the main idea of this reading? (Check the title and subtitles, look for illustrations, and read the first and last paragraphs to find main ideas.)

2. What do you already know about this topic? Make a quick list of ideas or words that come to mind.

3. Read the questions that follow the reading, and look for the answers as you read.

Now read the following passage.

Activism: Women, Chicanos, Indians

Women had been granted the vote in 1920 and for a time actively participated in politics and social reform movements. After this relatively brief period the women's movement became dormant, not to resurface until the 1960s. Yet during the decades in between the status of women underwent important changes. Some of the most significant occurred in the work force.

Source: Reprinted with permission of Macmillan Publishing Company from *An American Portrait* by David Burner *et. al.*, pages 785–792. Copyright © 1985 by David Burner.

WOMEN IN THE WORKPLACE

During the Depression working women were blamed for taking jobs from men, but women were not flooding the labor market and they earned fifty to sixty-five percent less than men. World War II altered the image of the working woman. More than one out of every three worked and almost half who did were married. For the first time the composite female worker was middled-aged, married, and a mother. Educated, white middle-class women were entering the work force in large numbers. Eleanor Roosevelt, by her active political involvement and extensive travels, exemplified a woman assuming new responsibilities.

The end of the war provoked a shift in attitudes. Woman was idealized as wife and mother, told to use newly acquired managerial skills to organize the household, arrange the carpools, and run the PTA. A post-war "baby boom" peaked in 1955. Maintaining their family's mental and physical well-being became a full-time commitment for many women; they adopted the identity of "supermom," a concept Betty Friedan termed "the feminine mystique."

Yet, the number of working women was higher than before the war, and continued to rise steadily. They were mainly working in occupations defined as female — clerical, domestic service, elementary school teaching; many other occupations, especially the professions, were increasingly restricted to men. Women were acquiring a smaller proportion of college degrees than they had forty years before. Still, by 1960 the number of working women was almost equal to that of men, and by the end of the decade almost nine out of every ten women, regardless of economic or social background, would be a part of the work force at some time in their lives.

The women's movement in the 1960s was closely related to the other reform movements of that period. The protest that the civil rights activists were raising against inequities in American life brought discrimination against women to public attention. And women, who found themselves relegated to secondary positions in the reform movements of the sixties, recognized that even reformism could reflect the injustices it was supposed to denounce. Stokely Carmichael, the militant black leader, once announced that "the only position for women in the movement is prone."

The first major recognition of the women's condition came when President Kennedy set up the President's Commission on the Status of Women in 1961. Its purpose was to investigate institutional discrimination against women and to provide concrete recommendations for change. The report confirmed that there was widespread discrimination, in both the public and the private sectors, and it urged the passage of new legislative and administrative laws. Title VII of the 1964 Civil Rights Act prohibited job discrimination because of race, color, religion, sex or national origin; it is still the most powerful legal tool women possess when fighting inequalities in work.

Literature was also probing the status of women. In 1953 Simone de Beauvoir's *The Second Sex*, tracing the subordination of women throughout history, had been published in the United States. In 1963 Betty Friedan wrote *The Feminine Mystique*, questioning the value and satisfaction middle-class women could derive from being housewives. This book, along with Kate Millett's *Sexual Politics* (1970) and Germaine Greer's *The Female Eunuch* (1971), had enormous impact on women. Also influential was an anthology of shorter writings by less prominent women entitled *Sisterhood is Powerful*, which presented important articles on housework, the psychology of women, marriage, minority-group women, and a broad range of other topics.

ORGANIZING POLITICALLY

Women formed their own groups to press for an end to discrimination. The National Organization of Women (NOW) was founded in 1966 with Friedan as its first president; it quickly became the largest and most influential women's group. From the beginning the local chapters were autonomous. NOW concentrated on legal challenges and nonpartisan political activity, allowed men to join, and functioned as an umbrella covering many disparate tendencies. NOW committed much of its energies to passage of the Equal Rights Amendment and to abortion rights. In 1963 the Women's Equity Action League was formed to lobby for legislation concerning women's work and education. Women's groups initiated national education campaigns to inform women of their rights and to explain the procedures used in fighting discrimination. Feminists have also been able to increase significantly their role in determining political party policies and goals. One of their most effective groups has been the national Women's Political Caucus, a nonpartisan group formed in 1971 to lobby for specific issues or candidates.

Women also carried the fight into state and federal courts, challenging statutes and practices that used sex as a legal classification. Three states now allow a husband to be prosecuted for raping his wife. Attention to these issues, along with others like the plight of battered wives and the need for child care services, have helped the movement reach women on all levels of society. Many activists avoided permanent organization, forming groups and caucuses to battle within universities, social welfare agencies, neighborhoods, hospitals, and places of employment. In 1973 both houses of Congress approved the Equal Rights Amendment, but it failed to gain the necessary ratification in three-fourths of the states.

In 1973 the Supreme Court handed down two decisions restricting the authority of states to prohibit abortion. The efforts of anti-abortionists to find other means of limiting the practice — federal legislation now allows medicaid funds only when the woman's life is in danger — made the defense of abortion rights a central issue for the women's movement. The arguments over abortion also reveal contrary tendencies within the movement. The woman's cause, like many of the other liberal and radical movements of recent times, has demanded absolute freedom in private life. But the left, with which the women's movement is allied, also called for the replacement of individualism with the virtues of community and cooperation. And at least a few advocates of women's rights have reacted against the idea of abortion on demand, proposing instead that society make it economically possible for women who wish to do so to have and bring up children. . . .

THE CHICANO MOVEMENT

Mexican-Americans, like other minorities, joined in the civil rights activism of the 1960s. Much of the movement originated among young Mexican-Americans who styled themselves "Chicanos" — a shortened term for Mexicano that had originated as a Mexican slang term to refer to a clumsy person. Chicanos sought control over their own educational, social and law enforcement institutions and demanded bilingual and bicultural education.

This movement had its antecedents. The League of United Latin American Citizens, formed in 1929, had won in 1945 a Supreme Court decision that began the demise of segregated education for Mexican-American children. The GI Forum fought discrimination in Texas. The Community Service Organization sought to register Mexican-American voters and solicit Mexican-American political candidates. The Mexican-American Political Association worked to marshal the Mexican-American vote so as to influence the two mainstream American political parties.

In part, the Chicano movement asserted whatever was distinctive to Mexican-American society. High school and college students in the Brown Berets staged walkouts for bilingual education. Activists called for Hispanic studies programs. Chicano culture gained recognition in theaters, among artists, and in the media. Alongside the celebration of cultural pluralism appeared separatist persuasions. The youthful urban-based Crusade for Justice, founded in Denver, Colorado, in 1965 by Rudalfo Gonzales, proposed that Chicanos reacquire the southwest as their own country. The group also sought jobs and social services for Mexican-Americans. The more rural *Alianza* (*Alianza Federal de Mercedes*, or Federal Alliance of Land Grants), founded by Reis Lopez Tyerina in 1963, demanded the return of millions of acres in the southwest to the descendants of those who had lost them despite guarantees in the Treaty of Guadalupe-Hidalgo. He hoped to establish a string of city-states. To implement his demands, the *Alianzas* occupied a court house in Tierra Amarillo, New Mexico, in 1967. After a massive manhunt, Tyerina was jailed in 1969, after which his movement declined.

More methodical politics also attracted activists. The La Raza Unida, founded in Texas under the leadership of José Angel Gutierrez in 1972, aimed to create a separate political party in control of local school boards and rural communities. While the movement gained momentum, it was unable to succeed in the cities. The renewal of the Voting Rights Act in 1975 strengthened Mexican-American political clout, as well as that of Indians and Asian-Americans. It provided for bilingual printing of ballots, voter pamphlets, and other political materials. Mexican-Americans soon won governorships in New Mexico and Arizona. Although most Mexican-Americans lived in cities, the most far-reaching and successful Chicano effort originated among migrant farm workers. Caesar Chavez, its leader, had also helped establish the Community Service Organization. As a youngster, he had attended more than thirty schools after his family lost their farm during the Depression. Migrant workers lived in camps, complete with drafty shanties and a few outdoor toilets and often a single water faucet for an entire camp. Committed like Martin Luther King to Gandhi's nonviolent tactics, and enlisting the support of the Roman Catholic hierarchy, Chavez has worked to organize the migrants, a portion of the nation's labor force so poor and so transient that unionism has hardly touched it.

Perhaps drawing on a page from the AFL handbook, Chavez concentrated on the most skilled migrant workers, the grape pickers. His United Farm Workers struck growers around Delano, California, in 1965. The union picketed and Chavez sought a nationwide boycott of grapes. In 1966, one company came to terms, including a wage of $1.75 per hour. Within two years, eleven growers had signed, giving a $2.25 wage and some benefits. Civil rights workers, young people, and ministers joined in support of Chavez's efforts. In 1968 Robert Kennedy's active support helped Chavez gain the national prominence the UFW needed, and by 1970, half of the hundred or more growers of table grapes came into line. Chavez then went after the lettuce growers but with less success. The Teamsters moved in and competed with the UFW for contracts. Agreement between the two unions failed and many growers swung over to the newer union. Finally, in 1977, the Teamsters gave the UFW the right to organize the field hands.

Like other immigrants, Mexican-Americans have struggled with the question of assimilation. Few immigrants came here to cease being what they were and to change their culture. As they accepted the new land and bought into its material style, they little understood

F I G U R E   3 . 3 Caesar Chavez (*Source:* © The Bettmann Archive)

what changes they needed in their cultural baggage to attain that style.

Nothing personifies the dilemma more than the bilingual question. Not only Anglo-Americans but Hispanics have divided over the issue. The Carter administration supported it; Reagan's has opposed it. Some argue that assimilation is inevitable and should take place sooner rather than later, so that the children of Hispanic parents will not be left indefinitely suspended between two languages and two cultures. Supporters of bilingual education argue that the maintenance of a Spanish-language alternative in public schools and other institutions, and thereby the sustenance of Mexican-American culture, will strengthen the pride of young Chicanos and ease the pain of transition for the current Mexican-American generation.

This issue will remain a significant one, for the closeness of the United States to Mexico and the openness of the border between the two countries virtually guarantees a reinforcement of old-country values for Mexican-American immigrants. Population projections reveal that Hispanic-Americans may become the most numerous minority in the United States sometime in the 1990s.

INDIAN ACTIVISM

The Dawes Severalty Act of 1887 had long since failed to assimilate American Indians. By the 1920s, whites had purchased much of the affected land, while other expanses among the original 160-acre tracts had been divided many times among the heirs and would not support Indian families even had they become farmers, as the act had intended. Demoralization attended high disease and infant mortality rates, unemployment, illiteracy, malnutrition, and alcoholism.

During the 1920s, reformers in the Indian Defense Association convinced John Collier, a student of Indian life, that the policy embodied in the Dawes Act needed to be reversed. When he became commissioner of Indian affairs under the New Deal, Collier used his studies, teaching and social work experience to produce the Wheeler-Howard Indian Reorganization Act (1934). This act sought to have Indians regain lost reservation lands and tribally manage their own affairs, as well as formal relations with local and national government. The act also promoted loans for reservation development and funded the training of Indians for hire by the Bureau of Indian Affairs. The Johnson-O'Malley Act, also passed in 1934, promoted the reclamation and irrigation of agricultural lands and the improvement of education and medical care. A number of Indian peoples, among them the Navahos, did not come under all of these programs. World War II, moreover, disrupted the programs while opening opportunities for employment off the reservation and for army enlistment. The military used Indian languages, notably Navaho, for wartime coded radio communications. During the war, Indian leaders founded the National Congress of American Indians, which at first represented over fifty tribes and eventually doubled in size. It was the first and largest nationwide Indian organization. While promoting educational employment and health services for Indians and lobbying Congress for beneficial laws, the National Congress sought to develop the reservation lands and resources and fought for Indian land claims against the government.

In the early 1950s, the relocation services program provided vocational and housing opportunities to Indians leaving their reservations. But most held unskilled city jobs and lived in wretched conditions. Many drifted back and forth between the city and the familiar and more communal reservation. The termination policy of 1953 completed for a moment the overturning of the policies that themselves had overturned the Dawes Act. It required a rapid end to federal support of some reservations. Indians charged that President Eisenhower was balancing his budget by violating treaty responsibilities and leaving the Indians exposed once again to unfriendly and impoverished state governments. They maintained that termination opened Indian lands to further exploitation by timber companies and land developers. The policy was soon abandoned and the government continued to struggle to develop a coherent and consistent Indian policy.

In 1961 over 400 Indians from nearly seventy tribes produced a "Declaration of Indian Purpose": self-determination, return of reservation lands, improvement of living conditions, and staffing the Bureau of Indian Affairs with Indians. And under Presidents Kennedy, Johnson, and Nixon the national government again advocated cultural pluralism for Indians. Johnson formed a national council on Indian opportunity, which reduced funds for training Indian workers for community and health services. Nixon appointed Louis Bruce, the first Indian Commissioner of Indian Affairs, and ordered that the bureau operate directly under presidential supervision to become more responsive to the problems of Indians.

In 1968, Dennis Banks and Clyde Bellecourt founded the American Indian Movement (AIM). That the organization began in Minneapolis reflected how urban the Indian experience was becoming. Of the 800,000 American Indians, approximately one-third now lived in cities. While AIM took up the cause of earlier reformers — reorganization of the Bureau, return of lands guaranteed by treaty, and Indian home rule — the tactics were much more militant. In 1969 Indians occupied the abandoned prison island of Alcatraz in San Francisco Bay. Led by a New York Mohawk, Richard Oakes, they demanded return of the island as partial payment for broken treaties. The publicity this event brought to the plight of urban Indians led to a series of Indian occupations of urban government property. In

1972, AIM members took over the main offices of the Indian Bureau in Washington, D.C. The most significant protest occurred at Wounded Knee in South Dakota, the site of the 1890 massacre of over 200 Sioux. Radical members of the Oglala Sioux and leaders of AIM seized and held the town. Led by Dennis Banks and Russell Means, they demanded the restoration of treaty lands. After seventy-one days and two deaths and several gunfights between the Indians and heavily armed National Guardsmen and FBI agents, the protesters surrendered. Over 300 were arrested. Most, including Banks and Means, were acquitted on legal technicalities.

Indians working within the system increasingly gained control over educational and commercial enterprises. By the end of the 1970s, Indians all over the country began lawsuits to recover their treaty rights and lands. In 1980 Washington Indians won rights to catch half of the salmon and steelhead in that state's rivers. The Nez Perce in Idaho worked on a cooperative settlement with the federal government to preserve declining runs of salmon. In Michigan, activists seeking to free Indians from state fishing regulations invoked treaty rights dating back to the 1830s.

In return for lost territory the government has usually paid in money rather than in land, though it returned almost 50,000 acres of forests to the Taos Indians in New Mexico. In 1972, it paid Alaskan Indians $925 million for claims to nearly 400 million acres and mineral rights. The Sioux received a settlement in 1978 of $44 million for 48 million acres and in 1979 of $105 million for 7 million acres of the Black Hills in South Dakota. In 1980, some Maine tribes, the Passamaquoddy, Penobscot, and Maliseet received over $54 million for purchase of 300,000 acres and a trust fund of half that amount for social welfare programs. Later in the year, they received $81.5 million more for their claims on 12 million acres.

Indian activism, in the face of the gain that it has won in rights and land claims, raises the very question on which it is founded: What does it mean to be Indian? Are Indians all one people or members of separate tribes? Can Indian culture be maintained on commercializing reservations or learned in city schools? Does an Indian who becomes a doctor or lawyer remain Indian? The very concept of Indian, of course, was meaningless before the Europeans and Africans, who defined as a single race the isolated or warring people of the western continent; yet modern generations of American Indians have sought to take their identity from those ancestors of the centuries preceding immigration from across the Atlantic. Perhaps it would be more useful to recognize "Indian" as referring to a comparatively recent, though very real culture and identity, created in conjunction with that other modern event, the United States.

A C T I V I T Y 7

Using information from the reading, answer the following questions.

Reading Questions

1. How did Title VII of the 1964 Civil Rights Act protect the rights of women, Hispanics, African-Americans, and Indians?

2. How did the renewal, in 1975, of the Voting Rights Act assist minority groups in attaining greater political power?

3. Why did some Indians benefit from World War II?

A C T I V I T Y 8

In your groups, discuss the following questions. Use information from the reading and lecture to help you answer them. Choose a spokesperson to report your answers to the class.

Reading Discussion Questions

1. Contrast the roles of working women during the Depression, World War II, and post World War II.

2. What is NOW, and how has it contributed to the political struggle of women?

3. What have native Americans (Indians) done to try to assert their rights? How has the American government responded?

4. Compare the work of Caesar Chavez and Martin Luther King, Jr. How did each man contribute to the civil rights movement?

5. What are some of the important similarities and differences in the United States among the civil rights movements of blacks, women, Chicanos, and Indians?

6. Which of the groups listed in question 5 do you think has fared the worst? the best? Why?

SKILL FOCUS ACTIVITY

ACTIVITY 9

Comparing and Contrasting

Comparing (showing the similarities) and contrasting (showing the differences) are two commonly used techniques in discussions and arguments for evaluating two items. These techniques are also a useful study skill, a way for students to organize information about different topics for purposes of answering essay questions that require the student to choose among alternative topics and justify his or her choice.

An example of an effective use of comparison and contrast in an argument follows:

> There are several reasons why the content-based approach is more effective than the cognitive approach to language learning for students who plan to study in U.S. universities or colleges. First, the content-based approach uses materials that are directly related to the goals of these students. For example, most content-based texts include readings from academic textbooks and scholarly works. In contrast, the materials used in the cognitive approach are generally adapted for second-language learners. Second, the content-based approach requires students to use the language to study other subjects, whereas the cognitive approach focuses on the study of the language itself. Finally, students in content-based classes develop academic language skills, which they will need in academic settings. The cognitive approach, however, develops students' basic interpersonal communication skills, which are important in everyday life, but insufficient to enable them to successfully participate in an academic environment.

In your group, choose two of the following groups, which you have read and talked about, and write a short talk comparing and contrasting them. Imagine your audience is other foreign students who know very little about the subject. Check your notes carefully so you do not make any inaccurate statements. Choose a spokesperson to present your group's speech to the class.

1. American Indians
2. Mexican-Americans
3. African-Americans
4. Women

HELPFUL VOCABULARY

The following transitional words and expressions are often used when comparing and contrasting.

CONTRAST	*COMPARISON*
unlike	so
but	like
however	the same _____ as
on the other hand	as
in contrast	similarly
not	in the same way

PROBLEM-SOLVING ACTIVITY

ACTIVITY 10

Discussion

In your groups, compare and contrast the problems faced by minority groups in your own societies with those faced by Americans. Some questions follow that you may want to consider in order to begin the discussion. Choose a spokesperson to report your answers to the class.

1. Do the laws in your country guarantee equal rights for all citizens, regardless of race, sex, color, or creed?

2. Are there any people in your country who are discriminated against by the majority group? What problems do the people who are discriminated against encounter?

3. What is the general attitude of people in your country toward "foreigners"?

4. Can you think of any solutions to the international problem of racism and discrimination?

EVALUATION ACTIVITIES

ACTIVITY 11

Test Review

Your teacher will distribute the study questions that your class wrote for this unit. In your groups, review your notes to make sure you have the information to answer the questions.

ACTIVITY 12

Test Correction

In your groups, review your answers to the test questions. If an answer is wrong, try to determine why and then try to find the correct answer. If you cannot determine why an answer is wrong, ask your teacher for assistance.

ACTIVITY 13

Answer the following questions concerning your experience working in your group. Be as explicit as you can. Only your teacher will read your answers, but you will be asked if you would like to share some of your answers in a class discussion.

Feedback Questionnaire

1. What kind of communication problems did your group encounter during the unit? How did you solve the problems?

2. Were all of your groups members in class every day? What happened to the group if someone was absent? What happened to the absentee group member when he or she came back?

3. Did your group usually stay on task? If not, what happened?

4. Did your group have a leader? What was the effect on the group of having a leader or of not having a leader?

5. What problems did your group encounter that may have been related to cultural differences? How did you solve the problems?

6. What did you learn about group dynamics from working in your group? What did you learn about yourself?

7. How did you contribute to the success or failure of your group?

8. What were some of the advantages of working in your group? What were some of the disadvantages?

9. What plans do you have to change your behavior in your next group? How will this change help you learn English better?

10. What suggestions do you have to give your teacher concerning the activities that your group completed in this unit?

UNIT
FOUR

Computer Science/
Problem Solving

Courtesy of International Business Machines Corporation

PREVIEW ACTIVITIES

Your teacher will divide your class into groups. These groups will remain the same throughout this unit.

ACTIVITY 1

The following preview problem is familiar. In your groups, try to solve it. List all the steps you followed to reach a solution. Choose a spokesperson to report your steps and solution to the class.

Preview Problem

Three missionaries and three cannibals must cross a river in a boat that holds only two people. The cannibals will eat the missionaries if they outnumber the missionaries on either bank of the river. How can six people cross the river and not have the cannibals eat the missionaries?

ACTIVITY 2

In your groups, try to determine the meanings of the following words. Do not use a dictionary. You will be comparing your definitions with those of the other groups, so take notes during your discussion. Choose a spokesperson to report your definitions to the class.

Lecture Vocabulary

1. manipulate	5. simulation	9. input
2. poll	6. exclusive of	10. output
3. woo	7. interchangeable	11. ascending
4. inventories	8. precisely	12. intervening

13. probable   16. irrelevant   18. memory
14. restriction 17. adjacent   19. arbitrary
15. penalty

| City X 1,345,987 | City Y 1,267,445 | City Z 1,114,256 |

FIGURE 4.1

CONTENT ACTIVITY: LECTURE

As you listen to the lectures on computer science and problem solving, take notes on what you hear. After each of the lectures, review your notes with your group members. After you have reviewed the notes, write the study questions that your teacher assigns.

ACTIVITY 3

Now that you have reviewed all your notes, in your group outline the lecture in the space provided. Focus on the organization of the lecture rather than on details. Choose a spokesperson to share your outline with the class.

Lecture Review Outline

  I. Introduction
 II. Types of Data or Information Processing
     A. Word Processing

III. Definitions

IV. Characteristics of Algorithms

V. Problem-Solving Techniques

VI. Problem-Solving Theory

VII. Problem-Solving Steps

SKILL FOCUS ACTIVITY

ACTIVITY 4

Analyzing Problems

As a student, you will have to analyze problems before you solve them, much like the computer programmer does. Correct analysis of the problem will contribute to a correct solution. Incorrect analysis will result in wrong solutions. Using ideas from the lecture for understanding problems, determine the initial and goal states of the following problems. Find any irrelevant information and look for constraints. Then solve the problem. Choose a spokesperson to report your group's analysis and solutions to the class. Be prepared to explain which problem-solving techniques you used.

PROBLEMS

1. You have a pine board that is 6 feet long. It weighs 8.5 pounds. You cut it into three pieces. Two are of equal length, and one is twice as long as one of the equal-length ones. Cut the longest piece of board in thirds and paint one piece blue. What fraction of the original board is left unpainted?

2. You want to frame a picture, which you purchased at an art gallery in New York, with some metal framing you bought. The picture measures 12½ inches by 7¾ inches. The framing is 54 inches long and 2 inches wide. How much framing will you have left after you cut the pieces necessary for the frame?

3. Mary needs to purchase a new pair of jeans, but her funds, as usual, are limited. Last week she had to spend $50.00 on car repairs. Three stores are having sales on sportswear, because it is the end of the season, and they need to make room for the new merchandise. Stores try to sell off leftover merchandise quickly to avoid large inventories. Store X is offering 35 percent off its $49.99 jeans, but the choice of sizes is limited because there are not many left. Store Y is offering only 25 percent off its $44.95 jeans, but there is a greater selection, almost 50 percent more. Store Z is offering a two-for-one sale on its $33.99 jeans. Where should Mary go to purchase the least expensive pair of jeans?

Now, in your groups write similar problems for other groups to solve. Include, where possible, irrelevant information and constraints. Make sure you know the initial state, goal state, and solutions for your problems.

CONTENT ACTIVITIES: READING

ACTIVITY 5

Answer the following questions *before* beginning to read "Errors and Loss Resulting from Criminal Activity."

Reading Preview Questions

1. What is the main idea of this reading? (Check the title and subtitles, look for illustrations, read the first and last paragraphs to find the main ideas.)

2. What do you already know about this topic? Make a quick list of ideas or words that come to mind.

3. Read the questions that follow the reading, and look for the answers as you read.

Now read the following passage.

Errors and Loss Resulting from Criminal Activity

Unintentional mistakes and equipment malfunction are not the only sources of computer error. Error caused by **criminal intrusion** into computer systems is a problem as well. Data needs to be pro-

Source: Reprinted with permission of Macmillan Publishing Company from *The Computer Challenge: Technology, Applications and Social Implications* by Donna S. Hussain and Khateeb M. Hussain, pp. 108–117. Copyright © 1986 by Macmillan Publishing Company.

tected against fraudulent changes, destruction, theft, and unauthorized disclosure.

Consider the billions of dollars involved in daily processing by computer. Every two to four hours, an estimated $845 billion is transferred electronically through computer networks. A person who taps into a computer can embezzle large sums of money. In one such case, an employee of Security Pacific National Bank got access to a money-transfer code and stole ten million dollars from the bank.

Data of a personal nature that is stored in a computer, such as health records and credit ratings, also needs protection. So does sensitive and proprietary information kept in computer memory. The theft of trade secrets, for example, can ruin a company's competitive advantage. Think of the value of formulas for petrochemical products. Advance knowledge of a competitor's new line (for example, Yves Saint-Laurent's spring fashions) or tampering with records (for example, altering student grades) can be harmful as well. Mervyn's department store was cheated out of $250,000 in merchandise by an employee who gained access to the store's computer to create phony credit card accounts. In 1983, ten Milwaukee youths were arrested for using home computers to gain access to a computer at the nuclear weapons research lab at Los Alamos, New Mexico. Although the accessed computer was not used for processing classified information, such an event certainly raises the issue of how safe computer systems really are. System security is an issue that is receiving much attention in computer circles and in the popular press today.

WHERE SECURITY IS NEEDED

Each stage of processing needs controls; that is, measures must be adopted to protect manuals, forms, files, and output. Data collection, data preparation, programming, and operations must also be monitored. . . .

Estimates of annual losses resulting from malice range from 100 million to 3 billion dollars. In a 1984 Computer Crime Task Force survey conducted by the American Bar Association, over 25 percent of the respondents reported "known and verifiable losses due to computer crime during the last twelve months"—losses that ranged between $145 and $730 million. (Per respondent, reported losses ranged from two million dollars to as high as ten million dollars.) An accurate assessment of total losses due to computer crime may never be achieved since many crimes are undetected. (Approximately 28 percent of the Bar Association survey respondents reported no available system to monitor or estimate the value of their computer crime losses.) Furthermore, many organizations do not report computer crimes because they are embarrassed that their security has been breached and fear that publicity will lead to loss of confidence in their management by the public.

PROTECTION AGAINST MALICE

Most of the control measures cited earlier in this chapter help protect computer systems from computer crime. But a number of measures specifically guard against criminal activity. **Physical access controls**, . . . which restrict a computer facility to authorized personnel, are one such measure. These controls may begin with perimeter security; that is, the property where the computer center is located may be protected by measures like fencing, alarms, cameras, lighting, a security force, patrols, and local police surveillance.

Physical barriers may also be installed at the computer center itself. Windows in the building may be barred and all exterior doors to the building kept locked and monitored by alarms, except for the lobby entrance where a security guard checks the authorization of people entering the building. TV monitors may watch entrances and motion detectors may be placed in sensitive areas. It is common practice to locate computer equipment in the most secure part of buildings, away from outside windows. A vault may be used to store data and files during nonworking hours.

Restricted entrance to computer equipment is another type of physical access control. Centers with tight security permit only operators, security officers, maintenance engineers, and system programmers in the computer room. These persons are required to wear badges and pass through a security station. Visitors are generally required to sign in and must be escorted by the persons they have come to visit.

To protect systems from employees with criminal intent who are bona fide computer users, an **access directory** stored in computer memory is customary. . . . Security codes needed to process specific data elements or files are listed in the directory. Before a job request is run, the CPU checks the directory to make sure that the user is authorized to use the programs and data required for the job. In other words, the codes restrict users to their work domain, preventing access to the files of others. Directories may also be used to specify which terminals can access the data base, the time of day access is permitted, and type of access, such as "read only" (meaning that files can be read by the user but not modified). THe use of secret **passwords** is still another control technique to limit access to data and files.

Teleprocessing adds to the problem of maintaining security. It is hard to restrict terminal use when terminals are scattered in remote locations. Moreover, data is subject to intrusion as it is transmitted over telecommunication lines to and from the CPU.

A number of sophisticated security techniques have been developed to protect the confidentiality of data during transmission. The implementation of **protocols** — that is, rules, conventions, and procedures governing computer access and user identification — is a major means of protecting system security. For example, a secret signal, called a **handshake**, may have to be received by the CPU before processing can begin. This prevents individuals from pretending to be legitimate users of the system when they are not.

Another common measure to prevent message interception is **data encryption**, or the coding of data. Encryption makes the data incomprehensible should wiretapping take place. In addition, security can be served by subdividing data messages into **packets** for transmission at different times of the day by a variety of routes.

Since studies show that employees within an organization are as likely to breach computer security with malicious intent as outsiders, . . . the **personnel policies** of an organization are very important. An organizational principle that contributes to computer security is **separation of responsibility**. Computing can be divided into five basic functions: programming and system development; handling input media; operation of data processing equipment; documentation and file library; and distribution of output. Under the principle of separation of responsibility, work assignments are designed so that employees do not have duties that cross these functional lines. For example, a person who helps develop a system does not operate it and certify results; a programmer who writes software does not input data and run the program. Separation of responsibility serves as a deterrent to

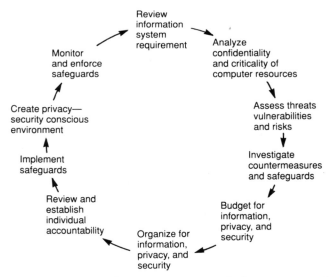

F I G U R E 4 . 2 An overview of the process of making a computer system secure. System security is a never ending cycle of planning, implementing, monitoring, and evaluating controls.

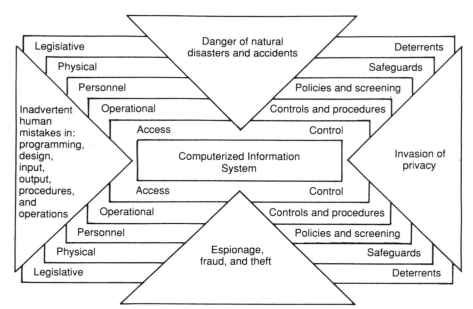

F I G U R E 4 . 3 Layers of protection. An information system is vulnerable to many types of threats to accuracy and system security. Many layers of protection are needed to counter these threats.

crime because a given job must pass through many hands, and there can thus be many independent checks for accuracy and possible fraud.

In small organizations, separation of responsibility may not be feasible. However, the principle should be followed whenever possible.

Care should also be taken in screening job applicants and in the supervision of employees. Workers should be technically competent and also trained in the vulnerability of computer systems. Awareness of the dimensions of computer crime can lead to more cautious use of computer resources.

In addition, employers should formulate and publicize conduct codes. They should encourage the formulation of ethical standards for computer users and professionals, and they should also provide forums for discussion of what these ethical standards should be. The Council of the Association for Computing Machinery and the Data Processing Management Association have adopted guidelines for professional conduct in information processing. The British Computer Society also has a code of conduct to which members are expected to subscribe. Other computer organizations, such as the American Federation for Information Processing Societies, have encouraged the development of codes of responsibility. Of course, codes can contribute to system security by serving as a framework for professional conduct, but they cannot be expected to eliminate ethical problems in computing altogether. Other professional groups with long-standing disciplinary procedures and enforcement mechanisms, such as the American Society of Civil Engineers, consider hundreds of ethical complaints every year.

The **law** can be another deterrent to crime. Unfortunately, legislatures move slowly. In a field as dynamic as computer science, the law simply hasn't kept pace with technological advances. As a result, a potpourri of statutes govern computer operations. More than forty sections of criminal code can be cited to provide sanctions for computer-related criminal conduct. Other applicable laws include the Wire Fraud Act, the Bank Fraud Acts, the Privacy Act, the Securities and Exchange Commission Insider Trading Rules, and the Foreign Corrupt Practices Act.

ACTIVITY 6

Using information from the reading, answer the following questions.

Reading Questions

1. What is computer crime?

2. List categories of security controls that can protect against computer crime, and give some examples for each category where appropriate.

A C T I V I T Y 7

In your groups, discuss the following questions. Use your answers from the reading questions to help you answer them. Choose a spokesperson to report your answers to the class.

Reading Discussion Questions

1. Which security controls seem most effective and why? For which particular computer crimes are they most effective?

2. Which security controls seem least effective and why? Against which computer crimes might they not be effective?

PROBLEM-SOLVING ACTIVITY

A C T I V I T Y 8

In your groups, discuss the following case study (problem). Make sure that you understand all of it. Using information from the reading and your knowledge of problem theory, define the problem and develop solutions. Choose a spokesperson to report your group's solutions to the class. Answers will vary, as there are numerous possible solutions.

Case Study: Security

David McCarthy has recently been hired by the SJQ company to develop and maintain computer security. The company manufactures bicycles at its main plant in Detroit and farm tractors and highly secret U.S. army tanks (the latter on contract from the U.S. government) at its plant in Dearborn. The company's administrative operations are fully automated, using standard data and word processing programs. The company is moving toward computer-aided manufacturing

(CAM), but at this time only a few of the production operations in the two factories are automated. The company, however, has recently added robots to the assembly line in the Dearborn factory. The engineering department is using computer-aided design (CAD) for simulations, particularly in the design and testing of the army tanks. Computers at both locations are connected in a star network, that is, all computers are connected to a main terminal, located at the plant in Detroit. What security measures should David McCarthy install to protect the company's records and activities, but still allow computer operations to function efficiently? Explain your choices.

SKILL FOCUS ACTIVITY

ACTIVITY 9

Presenting Research Results

As a student, you may be required to do research on an academic topic and to present the results of that research orally to a class. Academic speakers report the results of their research. They tell the audience what they studied, how they studied it (i.e., the methods they used), the results of their study, and their evaluation of the results. Good academic speakers organize their material well and give clear explanations.

One of the most common formats for presenting research is the academic panel. On an academic panel, several different researchers present the results of their work. Although each speaker's presentation may be very specific, the panel topic is generally broad enough to cover all the different presentations. After all the researchers have spoken, the audience is expected to ask questions and to discuss the information. All speakers must be prepared to answer questions from the audience on any part of their presentation.

In your group, choose one of the following topics to research.

1. How to protect against computer fraud.
2. How to best learn a second language.
3. How to control population growth.
4. How to eliminate discrimination.

Develop a questionnaire on the topic: write questions that, when they are answered, will provide data on the respondents' ideas of what the problem is, what the solution is, what the steps required to reach the solution are, and what the advantages and disadvantages of the solution are. Interview at least 16 people, 3 or 4 per group member. After you have completed the interviewing process, analyze the results.

Prepare a panel presentation of your results to give to the class. One member of the group reports on what the respondents considered the problem to be, that is, the respondents' definitions of the problem (their idea of the initial state). A second group member reports on what the respondents considered the solution to be, that is, the respondents' opinions of the best solution (their idea of the goal state). A third group member reports on what the respondents considered to be the best sequence of steps to take in order to arrive at a solution. The fourth group member reports on what the respondents considered to be the advantages and disadvantages of their solutions. In a four-member group, this person also moderates the panel by introducing the panel members and directing audience questions to the appropriate panel member. Each speaker explains the questions from the questionnaire that pertain to his or her topic and describes the responses to those questions collected by group members. Each person speaks for about 7 to 10 minutes. The audience's responsibility is to ask questions about the research.

HELPFUL VOCABULARY

I would like to introduce our panel. On my right (left) is _____.

Mr. _____ will discuss _____.

The results of our research show (indicate) that _____.

If you look at these responses, you will see _____.

_____ percent answered that _____.

Of the _____ responses, only _____ indicated _____.

Most respondents felt that _____.

EVALUATION ACTIVITIES

A C T I V I T Y 10

Test Review

Your teacher will distribute the study questions that your class wrote for this unit. In your groups, review your notes to make sure you have the information to answer the questions.

A C T I V I T Y 11

Test Correction

In your groups, review your answers to the test questions. If an answer is wrong, try to determine why and then try to find the correct answer. If you cannot determine why an answer is wrong, ask your teacher for assistance.

A C T I V I T Y 12

Answer the following questions concerning your experience working in your group. Be as explicit as you can. Only your teacher will read your answers, but you will be asked if you would like to share some of your answers in a class discussion.

Feedback Questionnaire

1. What kind of communication problems did your group encounter during the unit? How did you solve the problems?

2. Were all of your group members in class every day? What happened to the group if someone was absent? What happened to the absentee group member when he or she came back?

3. Did your group usually stay on task? If not, what happened?

4. Did your group have a leader? What was the effect on the group of having a leader or of not having a leader?

5. What problems did your group encounter that may have been related to cultural differences? How did you solve the problems?

6. What did you learn about group dynamics from working in your group? What did you learn about yourself?

7. How did you contribute to the success or failure of your group?

8. What were some of the advantages of working in your group? What were some of the disadvantages?

9. What plans do you have to change your behavior in your next group? How will this change help you learn English better?

10. What suggestions do you have to give to your teacher concerning the activities that your group completed in this unit?

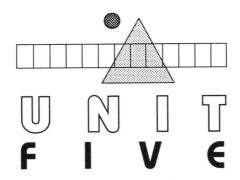

UNIT
FIVE

Motivation

PREVIEW ACTIVITIES

Your teacher will divide your class into groups. These groups will remain the same throughout the unit.

ACTIVITY 1

Scenarios

Each group will receive one copy of a scenario role, and your group will have 10 to 15 minutes to prepare for this activity.

ACTIVITY 2

After your class has rehearsed, performed, and discussed the scenarios, complete the following exercise.

Student Scenario Worksheet

1. *Vocabulary and idioms.* Write here as many of the new words as you can remember from today's scenarios.

2. *Topic and roles.* What was the topic of each scenario? Write a brief description of the different roles performed by the students, and include a description of the performers' goals.

3. *Strategies.* How did the student performers try to accomplish their goals? What particular strategies were most effective? Who had the most control of the conversations? Why?

4. *Structures.* Write examples of new constructions you learned today. What grammar points are illustrated?

A C T I V I T Y 3

In your groups, discuss the following question. Gather as many answers as possible from group members. Choose a spokesperson to report your ideas to the class.

Preview Discussion

Imagine that you are the manager in a factory or office. What do you think motivates your employees to work? What could you do to make them work harder or better?

A C T I V I T Y 4

In your groups, try to determine the meanings of the following words. Do not use a dictionary. You will be comparing your definitions with those of the other groups, so take notes during your discussion. Choose a spokesperson to report your definitions to the class.

Lecture Vocabulary

1. fulfill
2. hierarchy
3. instrumentality
4. divert
5. pension

6. prestige
7. status
8. promotion
9. reward
10. probability

11. equitable
12. expend
13. premise
14. physiological

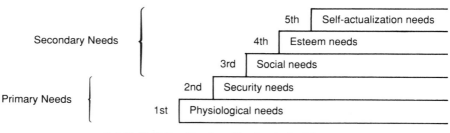

F I G U R E 5 . 1 Maslow's ladder

The Theoretical Model

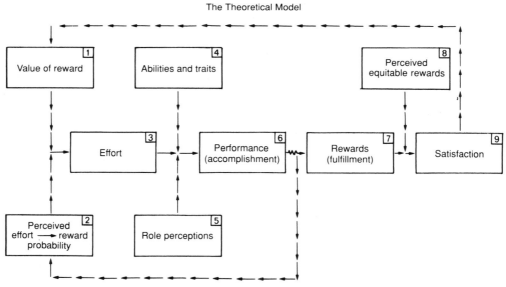

F I G U R E 5 . 2 Porter-Lawler model. *Source:* Porter, Lyman W., and Edward E. Lawler, *Managerial Attitudes and Performance* (Homewood, Illinois: Richard D. Irwin, Inc.), 1968, p. 17. Reprinted by permission from the publisher.

CONTENT ACTIVITY: LECTURE

As you listen to the lectures on motivation, take notes on what you hear. After each of the lectures, review your notes with your group members. After you have reviewed the notes, write the study questions that your teacher assigns.

ACTIVITY 5

Now that you have reviewed all your notes in your group, outline the lecture in the space provided. Focus on the organization of the lecture rather than on details. Choose a spokesperson to share your outline with the class.

Lecture Review Outline

I. Introduction

II. Maslow Model

III. Porter-Lawler Model

SKILL FOCUS ACTIVITY

A C T I V I T Y 6

Defining Terms and Concepts

Definitions are an essential part of academic discourse. Definitions are used to indicate clearly and exactly what a term (word) or a concept means in the context of a lecture or reading. In college and university courses, students must know the specific definitions of terms or concepts used by the instructor and the textbook, not only to understand course information, but also to pass exams. Multiple choice and true/false questions often test students' knowledge of definitions. Short answer questions require students to give definitions. Essay questions may also include definitions.

Some academic definitions are short, for example:

> The term *democracy* comes from two Greek words: *demos*, meaning people, and *kratis*, meaning rule or government. Democracy means government or rule by the people, as compared with *autocracy*, rule by one.

Other academic definitions, especially those of concepts, can be much longer or extended, for example:

> Democracy, as a system, focuses on control of the rulers by the ruled. The rulers are officials of governments elected by the people in competitive elections. Voters control their elected representatives by holding over them the possibility of removal from office if the representatives fail to pursue government policies that reflect the wishes of the majority. Safeguards for individual and minority rights against majorities are embodied in constitutions, laws, court decisions, and customs. Argument and competing parties are the core of democracy. Democracies can be subverted if the public is denied access to information. If news media do not inform voters of problems and policy options with clear focused expert arguments about problems, then the voters lack an adequate basis for choosing and holding their representatives accountable.

Extended definitions limit and clearly specify how a term or a concept will be used in a particular context. The definition may include reasons or arguments, descriptions of processes, examples, comparisons, and so on. In the previous definition, the writer uses the example of the role of the news media to focus on how the ruled control the rulers through informed choice in a democracy.

In your groups, choose two of the following terms, which were defined and used in the lecture, and give both a short and an extended definition. Create your own examples, comparisons, descriptions, and so on. Do not use examples from the lecture. Choose a spokesperson to present your group's definitions to the class.

needs	prestige	status
reward	effort	esteem needs
role perceptions	performance	satisfaction

HELPFUL VOCABULARY

As used here _____ means _____.

In this context _____ is defined as _____.

Let me first explain what I mean by _____.

In a narrow sense _____ means _____.

An example of _____ is _____.

_____ is similar to (different from) _____.

CONTENT ACTIVITIES: READING

ACTIVITY 7

Reading Preview Questions

Answer the following questions *before* beginning to read "The Functions of Work."

1. What is the main idea of this textbook reading? (Check the title and subtitle, look for illustrations, and read the first and last paragraphs to find main ideas.)

2. What do you already know about this topic? Make a quick list of ideas or words that come to mind.

3. Read the questions that follow the reading, and look for the answers as you read.

Now read the following passage.

*The Functions of Work**

The economic purposes of work are obvious and require little comment. Work is the means by which we provide the goods and services needed and desired by ourselves and our society. Through the economic rewards of work, we obtain immediate gratification of transient wants, physical assets for enduring satisfactions, and liquid assets for deferrable gratifications. For most of the history of mankind, and for a large part of humanity today, the economic meaning of work is paramount.

Work also serves a number of other social purposes. The workplace has always been a place to meet people, converse, and form friendships. In traditional societies, where children are wont to follow in their parents' footsteps, the assumption of responsibility by the children for one task and then another prepares them for their economic and social roles as adults. Finally, the type of work performed has always conferred a social status on the worker and the worker's family. In industrial America, the father's occupation has been the major determinant of status, which in turn has determined the family's class standing, where they lived, where the children went to school, and with whom the family associated—in short, the life style and life chances of all the family members. (The emerging new role of women in our society may cause class standing to be co-determined by the husband's *and* wife's occupations.)

The economic and societal importance of work has dominated thought about its meaning, and justifiably so: a function of work for

*Footnotes omitted.

Source: Special Task Force to Secretary of Health, Education, and Welfare, *Work in America* (Cambridge, Massachusetts: MIT Press), 1973, pp. 2–7. Reprinted by permission.

any *society* is to produce and distribute goods and services, to transform "raw nature" into that which serves our needs and desires. Far less attention has been paid to the *personal* meaning of work, yet it is clear from recent research that work plays a crucial and perhaps unparalleled psychological role in the formation of self-esteem, identity, and a sense of order.

Work contributes to self-esteem in two ways. The first is that, through the inescapable awareness of one's efficacy and competence in dealing with the objects of work, a person acquires a sense of mastery over both himself and his environment. The second derives from the view, stated earlier, that an individual is working when he is engaging in activities that produce something valued by other people. That is, the job tells the worker day in and day out that he has something to offer. Not to have a job is not to have something that is valued by one's fellow human beings. Alternatively, to be working is to have evidence that one is needed by others. One of these components of self-esteem (mastery) is, therefore, internally derived through the presence or absence of challenge in work. The other component (how others value one's contributions) is externally derived. The person with high self-esteem may be defined as one who has a high estimate of his value and finds that the social estimate agrees.

The workplace generally, then, is one of the major foci of personal evaluation. It is where one finds out whether he is "making the grade"; it is where one's esteem is constantly on the line, and where every effort will be made to avoid reduction in self-evaluation and its attending sense of failure. If an individual cannot live up to the expectations he has of himself, and if his personal goals are not reasonably obtainable, then his self-esteem, and with it his relations with others, are likely to be impaired.

Doing well or poorly, being a success or failure at work, is all too easily transformed into a measure of being a valuable or worthless human being, as Erich Fromm writes:

> Since modern man experiences himself both as the seller and as the commodity to be sold on the market, his self-esteem depends on conditions beyond his control. If he is successful, he is valuable; if he is not, he is worthless.

When it is said that work should be "meaningful," what is meant is that it should contribute to self-esteem, to the sense of fulfillment through the mastering of one's self and one's environment, and to the sense that one is valued by society. The fundamental question the individual worker asks is "What am I doing that *really* matters?"

When work becomes merely automatic behavior, instead of being *homo faber*, the work is *animal laborens*. Among workers who describe themselves as "just laborers," self-esteem is so deflated that the distinction between the human as worker and animal as laborer is blurred. The relationship between work and self-esteem is well summarized by Elliot Jacques:

> . . . working for a living is one of the basic activities in a man's life. By forcing him to come to grips with his environment, with his livelihood at stake, it confronts him with the actuality of his personal capacity—to exercise judgment, to achieve concrete and specific results. It gives him a continuous account of his correspondence between outside reality and the inner perception of that reality, as well as an account of the accuracy of his appraisal of himself. . . . In short, a man's work does not satisfy his material needs alone. In a very deep sense, it gives him a measure of his sanity.

Work is a powerful force in shaping a person's sense of identity. We find that most, if not all, working people tend to describe themselves in terms of the work groups or organizations to which they belong. The question, "Who are you?" often solicits an organizationally related response, such as "I work for IBM," or "I'm a Stanford professor." Occupational role is usually a part of this response for all classes: "I'm a steelworker," or "I'm a lawyer." In short: "People tend to 'become what they do.'"

Several highly significant effects result from work-related identification: welfare recipients become "nobodies"; the retired suffer a crucial loss of identity; and people in low-status jobs either cannot find anything in their work from which to derive an identity or they reject the identity forced on them. Even those who voluntarily leave an organization for self-employment experience difficulties with identity—compounded by the confusion of others—as the following quote from an article entitled "Striking Out on Your Own" illustrates:

> No less dramatic . . . are those questions of identity which present themselves to the self-employed. These identity crises and situations usually come packaged in little episodes which occur when others find that they have encountered a bona fide weirdo without a boss. . . . You are stopped by a traffic policeman to be given a ticket and he asks the name of your employer and you say that you work for yourself. Next he asks, "Come on, where do you work? Are you employed or not?" You say, "Self-employed." . . . He, among others you meet, knows that self-employment is a tired euphemism for being out of work. . . . You become extremely nervous about meeting new people because of the ever-present question, "Who are you with?" When your answer fails to attach you to a recognized organization . . . both

parties to the conversation often become embarrassed by your obscurity.

Basic to all work appears to be the human desire to impose order, or structure, on the world. The opposite of work is not leisure or free time; it is being victimized by some kind of disorder which, at its extreme, is chaos. It means being unable to plan or to predict. And it is precisely in the relation between the desire for order and its achievement that work provides the sense of mastery so important to self-esteem. The closer one's piece of the world conforms with one's structural plans, the greater the satisfaction of work. And it follows that one of the greatest sources of dissatisfaction in work results from the inability to make one's own sense of order prevail—the assembly line is the best (or worst) example of an imposed, and, for most workers, unacceptable structure.

ACTIVITY 8

Using information from the reading, answer the following questions.

Reading Questions

1. What are some of the economic, social, and psychological purposes of work?

2. How does work contribute to a person's psychological self-esteem, identity, and sense of order? Give examples.

3. Give examples (other than those listed in the article) to support the premise that "people tend to become what they do."

ACTIVITY 9

Answer the following questions *before* beginning to read "Arthur Friedman's Outrage: Employees Decide Their Pay."

Reading Preview Questions

1. What is the main idea of this newspaper reading? (Check the title, scan the first three and the last paragraphs to find main ideas.)

2. Read the questions that follow the reading, and look for answers as you read.

Now read the following passage.

Arthur Friedman's Outrage:
Employees Decide Their Pay

OAKLAND, Calif. — One thing for sure, Arthur Friedman will never become the chairman of the board at General Motors.

It is not just because the modish, easygoing Oakland appliance dealer does not look the part — Hush Puppies, loud shirts and denim jackets tend to clash with the sober decor of most executive suites. And it certainly is not because he is an incompetent administrator — the Friedman-Jacobs Co. has prospered during the 15 years of his stewardship.

It is mainly because Art Friedman has some pretty strange ideas about how one runs a business.

Five years ago, he had his most outrageous brainstorm. First he tried it out on his wife Merle and his brother Morris.

"Here he goes again," replied Merle with a sigh of resignation. "Another dumb stunt."

"Oh my God," was all that Morris could muster.

His idea was to allow employees to set their own wages, make their own hours and take their vacations whenever they felt like it.

The end result was that it worked.

Friedman first unleashed his proposal at one of the regular staff meetings. Decide what you are worth, he said, and tell the bookkeeper to put it in your envelope next week. No questions asked. Work any time, any day, any hours you want. Having a bad day? Go home. Hate working Saturdays? No problem. Aunt Ethel from Chicago has dropped in unexpectedly? Well, take a few days off, show her the town. Want to go to Reno for a week, need a rest? Go, go, no need to ask. If you need some money for the slot machines, take it out of petty cash. Just come back when you feel ready to work again.

His speech was received in complete silence. No one cheered, no one laughed, no one said a word.

"It was about a month before anyone asked for a raise," recalls Stan Robinson, 55, the payroll clerk. "And when they did, they asked Art first. But he refused to listen and told them to just tell me what they wanted. I kept going back to him to make sure it was all right, but he wouldn't even talk about it. I finally figured out he was serious."

"It was something that I wanted to do," explains Friedman. "I always said that if you give people what they want, you get what you want. You have to be willing to lose, to stick your neck out. I finally decided that the time had come to practice what I preached."

Source: "Arthur Friedman's Outrage: Employees Decide Their Pay," by Martin Koughan, *Washington Post*, February 23, 1975, p. C-1. Reprinted with permission.

Soon the path to Stan Robinson's desk was heavily travelled. Friedman's wife Merle was one of the first; she figured that her contribution was worth $1 an hour more. Some asked for $50 more a week, some $60. Delivery truck driver Charles Ryan was more ambitious; he demanded a $100 raise.

In most companies, Ryan would have been laughed out of the office. His work had not been particularly distinguished. His truck usually left in the morning and returned at 5 in the afternoon religiously, just in time for him to punch out. He dragged around the shop, complained constantly and was almost always late for work. Things changed.

"He had been resentful about his prior pay," explains Friedman. "The raise made him a fabulous employee. He started showing up early in the morning and would be back by 3, asking what else had to be done."

Instead of the all-out raid on the company coffers that some businessmen might expect, the 15 employees of the Friedman-Jacobs Co. displayed astonishing restraint and maturity. The wages they demanded were just slightly higher than the scale of the Retail Clerks union to which they all belong (at Friedman's insistence). Some did not even take a raise. One service man who was receiving considerably less than his co-workers was asked why he did not insist on equal pay. "I don't want to work that hard," was the obvious answer.

When the union contract comes across Friedman's desk every other year, he signs it without even reading it. "I don't care what it says," he insists. At first, union officials would drop in to see how things were going, but they would usually end up laughing and shaking their heads, muttering something about being put out of a job. They finally stopped coming by. It was enough to convince George Meany to go out to pasture.

The fact is that Friedman's employees have no need for a union; whatever they want, they take and no one questions it. As a result they have developed a strong sense of responsibility and an acute sensitivity to the problems that face the American worker in general that would have been impossible under the traditional system.

George Tegner, 59, an employee for 14 years, has like all his co-workers achieved new insight into the mechanics of the free enterprise system. "You have to use common sense; no one wins if you end up closing the business down. If you want more money, you have to produce more. It can't work any other way. Anyway, wages aren't everything. Doing what you want to is more important."

Roger Ryan, 27, has been with the company for five years. "I know about the big inflation in '74, but I haven't taken a raise since '73. I figure if everybody asks for more, then inflation will just get worse. I'll hold out as long as I can."

Payroll clerk Stan Robinson: "I'm single now. I don't take as much as the others even though I've been here longer, because I don't need as much. The government usually winds up with the extra money anyway."

Elwood Larsen, 65, has been the company's ace service man for 16 years. When he went into semi-retirement last year, he took a $1.50 cut in pay. Why? Larsen does not think a part-timer is worth as much. "I keep working here because I like it. We all know that if the Friedmans make money, we do. You just can't gouge the owner."

In the past five years, there has been no turnover of employees. Friedman estimates that last year his 15 workers took no more than a total of three sick days. It is rare that anyone is late for work and, even then, there is usually a good reason. Work is done on time and employee pilferage is nonexistent.

"We used to hear a lot of grumbling," says Robinson. "Now, everybody smiles."

As part of the new freedom, more people were given keys to the store and the cash box. If they need groceries, or even some beer money, all they have to do is walk into the office, take what they want out of the cash box and leave a voucher. Every effort is made to ensure that no one looks over their shoulder.

There has been only one discrepancy. "Once the petty cash was $10 over," recalls Friedman. "We never could figure out where it came from."

The policy has effected some changes in the way things are done around the store. It used to be open every night and all day Sunday, but no one wanted to work those hours. A problem? Of course not. No more nights and Sundays. ("When I thought about it," confesses Friedman, "I didn't like to work those hours either.")

The store also used to handle TVs and stereos—high-profit items—but they were a hassle for all concerned. The Friedman-Jacobs Co. now deals exclusively in major appliances such as refrigerators, washers and dryers.

Skeptics by now are chuckling to themselves, convinced that if Friedman is not losing money, he is just breaking even. The fact is that net profit has not dropped a cent in the last five years; it has increased. Although volume is considerably less and overhead has increased at what some would consider an unhealthy rate, greater productivity and efficiency have more than made up for it.

ACTIVITY 10

Using information from the readings, answer the following questions.

Reading Questions

1. What did Arthur Friedman do five years ago?

2. How did Arthur Friedman's actions motivate his employees?

3. How did Arthur Friedman's actions affect his company's performance?

ACTIVITY 11

In your groups, discuss the following questions. Use your answers from the reading questions to help you answer them. Choose a spokesperson to report your answers to the class.

Reading Discussion Questions

1. What kinds of work might not contribute to self-esteem, identity, and a sense of order? Why?

2. According to the first article, the opposite of work is not leisure. What is the opposite of work and why? Do you agree? If so, why? If not, why not?

3. How are the Maslow and Porter-Lawler models illustrated by these articles? Give specific examples.

PROBLEM-SOLVING ACTIVITY

ACTIVITY 12

Discussion

In your groups, discuss whether the Maslow and Porter-Lawler models are applicable to your own societies and cultures. Following are some questions you might want to consider in order to begin the discussion. Choose a spokesperson to report your answers to the class.

1. In some societies, physiological and safety needs are satisfied by the state; that is, housing and jobs are guaranteed to all citizens. Does that fact weaken or destroy work motivation? Why?

2. In some societies, employees work for a company for their entire career, and even social needs are met by the company. Does this fact make the models under consideration here less valid for these societies? Why?

3. In some countries, labor is in great supply; in other countries there is a shortage of labor. How might the labor supply affect the efforts of managers to motivate employees?

SKILL FOCUS ACTIVITY

A C T I V I T Y 13

Applying Information to New Situations or Problems

In college or university courses, students acquire knowledge that they then must apply to new situations or use to solve new problems. Exams, particularly in mathematics, the sciences, and business administration, have numerous application problems. In the following exercise you are asked to solve a management problem. First read the case study (the problem) and discuss it with your group. Be sure you understand all of it before you begin to answer the question. Using the information about work, the Maslow model, and the Porter-Lawler model, solve Joe McLean's problem. Choose a spokesperson to report your solutions to the class. Not all groups will have the same answers, as there are numerous possible solutions.

Case Study: Convention Sales

Joe McLean, age 36, was hired six months ago as manager of convention sales for a hotel in a large east coast city. Previously he was advertising sales manager for a local television station. The hotel itself was acquired last year by a major hotel chain. The hotel has a convention center of six meeting rooms, a large auditorium that can be used for expositions, and several restaurants. As manager, Joe was required to participate in two of the chain's training seminars on techniques for increasing sales of convention space and services. These seminars emphasized the team approach to sales, and Joe decided that his sales staff would adopt this approach. However, his staff of four, all of whom are over the age of 42, have worked with convention sales for the past five years on a commission* basis and have each developed their own list of clients. They also have received sometimes substantial annual bonuses based on the total amount of individual sales. What can Joe do to motivate his staff to adopt the team approach to sales?

---

*A commission is an amount of money earned by a salesperson based on his or her total sales.

HELPFUL VOCABULARY

_____ should _____ because _____.

If you assume that _____, then _____.

Obviously, _____. So _____.

Personally I believe _____.

Using the _____ model _____.

There are several reasons why _____.

In the first (second, third) place _____.

PROBLEM-SOLVING ACTIVITY

A C T I V I T Y 14

Computing Motivation Potential

Supervisors are sometimes inefficient in their efforts to motivate employees because they choose rewards that are not important to the employee or because the employees want rewards over which supervisors have no control. Effective motivation can only be accomplished if rewards desired and offered are properly integrated.

We can view motivation potential (*MP*) as a function of two major variables: (1) employee needs (or wants, drives, goals, and so on) and how important these needs are (*NI*), and (2) how much control the supervisor has over these needs (*C*). We can express this relationship mathematically as follows:

$$MP = (NI) \times (C)$$

Imagine that your group members are supervisors of a company. The following steps can be used to compute the motivational potential of your employees.

1. In your group, create a list of what rewards motivate employees.

2. Imagine that your employees are another class group. Interview

Source: Quoted and adapted from Jerry L. Gray, *Supervision: An Applied Behavioral Science Approach to Managing People* (Boston: Kent Publishing Co., 1984), pp. 165–166. Copyright © by Wadsworth, Inc. Reprinted and adapted by permission of PWS-KENT Company, a division of Wadsworth, Inc.

each group member and ask him or her to rank order the items (rewards) on your list. (*Rank order* means to list the items in the order of their importance.) Assign each item a value on a scale of zero to ten, ten representing high importance and zero representing no importance.

3. In your group, assign another value to each item showing how much control you, as supervisor, have over it. Use a scale of zero to ten again, ten representing a high degree of control and zero representing no control. For example, if one of the items is six weeks of vacation annually, and the company gives only a maximum of four weeks, you would assign that item a value of zero. Because you cannot give six weeks of vacation, you have no control over this item.

4. Using the formula, you can compute the motivational potential of each item. You now have a numerical figure that gives you the item(s) that have the highest motivation potential. This tells you how you should direct your efforts. Obviously, there is little value in spending time attempting to motivate someone who is motivated by something beyond your control. Although every situation is relative, you should generally concentrate on items that have a net value of about 50 or higher. Table 5.1 shows an example of how this system is used in a hypothetical case.

5. Choose a spokesperson to report your group's results to the class.

TABLE 5.1 Example of the Computational Approach to Motivation

(EN) EMPLOYEE NEED	(NI)* NEED IMPORTANCE	(SC)* SUPERVISORY CONTROL	(MP) MOTIVATIONAL POTENTIAL
More money	(7)	(4)	28
Promotion	(6)	(4)	24
Group acceptance	(9)	(2)	18
Better working conditions	(4)	(6)	24
Longer vacation	(7)	(0)	○
Less supervision	(8)	(9)	(72)
More responsibility	(8)	(7)	56
Better pension plan	(7)	(0)	○
More power	(5)	(2)	10
Better interpersonal relations	(9)	(3)	27

*Items are measured on a scale of zero (low) to ten (high).
○ indicates motivation source with greatest potential.

EVALUATION ACTIVITIES

ACTIVITY 15

Test Review

Your teacher will distribute the study questions that your class wrote for this unit. In your groups, review your notes to make sure that you have the information to answer the questions.

ACTIVITY 16

Test Correction

In your groups, review your answers to the test questions. If an answer is wrong, try to determine why and then try to find the correct answer. If you cannot determine why an answer is wrong, ask your teacher for assistance.

ACTIVITY 17

Answer the following questions concerning your experience working in your group. Be as explicit as you can. Only your teacher will read your answers, but you will be asked if you would like to share some of your answers in a class discussion.

Feedback Questionnaire

1. What kind of communication problems did your group encounter during the unit? How did you solve the problems?

2. Were all of your group members in class every day? What happened to the group if someone was absent? What happened to the absentee group member when he or she came back?

3. Did your group usually stay on task? If not, what happened?

4. Did your group have a leader? What was the effect on the group of having a leader or of not having a leader?

5. What problems did your group encounter that may have been related to cultural differences? How did you solve the problems?

6. What did you learn about group dynamics from working in your group? What did you learn about yourself?

7. How did you contribute to the success or failure of your group?

8. What were some of the advantages of working in your group? What were some of the disadvantages?

9. What plans do you have to change your behavior in your next group? How will this change help you learn English better?

10. What suggestions do you have to give to your teacher concerning the activities that your group completed in this unit?

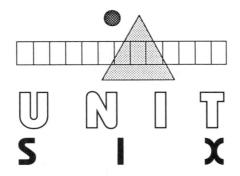

UNIT SIX

The Evolution of Stars

© The Bettmann Archive

PREVIEW ACTIVITIES

Your teacher will divide your class into groups. These groups will remain the same throughout the unit.

ACTIVITY 1

Preview Problem

In your groups, complete the following task. Imagine that you are a group of microbiologists who have been chosen by your government to assist in a top secret assignment. Recently, a space probe was sent to a distant planet and returned to earth with samples from the planet surface. The government has asked you to classify the samples, so that similarities and differences in their structure can be studied. Figure 6.1 illustrates the 12 samples to be classified.

Your task is to sort the objects into categories and to define the criteria you used to sort them. Choose a group secretary to write down the criteria you identify for each step in your analysis. First, divide the objects into two groups, looking for general criteria. Then subdivide those two groups into four groups, and write down the new criteria. Finally, subdivide two groups once more, so you will end up with a total of six groups. Write down the final criteria for the six groups you have identified. Choose a spokesperson to report your selections and criteria for those selections to the class.

ACTIVITY 2

In your groups, discuss the following questions. Gather as many answers from your group members as possible. Choose a spokesperson to report your ideas to the class.

Preview Discussion

1. What is a star? Why do stars shine?

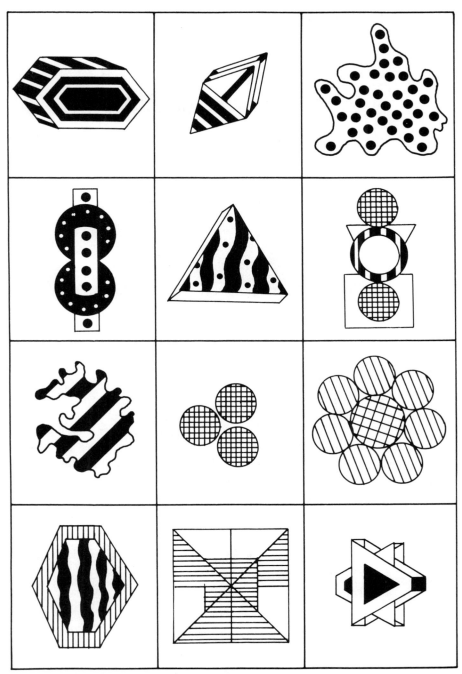

F I G U R E   6 . 1   Samples from surface of Planet X (*Source:* © John Schneider)

2. How is a star born? How does it die?

3. What do astronomers do? What tools help them in their research?

4. How do astronomers classify stars?

5. What would you like to learn about stars?

A C T I V I T Y 3

In your groups, try to determine the meanings of the following words. Do not use a dictionary. You will be comparing your definitions with those of the other groups, so take notes during your discussion. Choose a spokesperson to report your definitions to the class.

Lecture Vocabulary

1. emit
2. fuse (v)
3. contract (v)
4. expand
5. stellar
6. envelope (n)
7. electron
8. degenerate (v)
9. pulse (v)
10. remnant
11. particle
12. radiation
13. matter
14. convert (v)
15. paradox
16. celestial

Note: The following terms will be defined in the lecture. Listen and record the definitions after each part of the lecture.

1. stellar astronomy   4. neutron star   7. black hole
2. spectrum   5. red giant   8. pulsar
3. luminosity   6. white dwarf

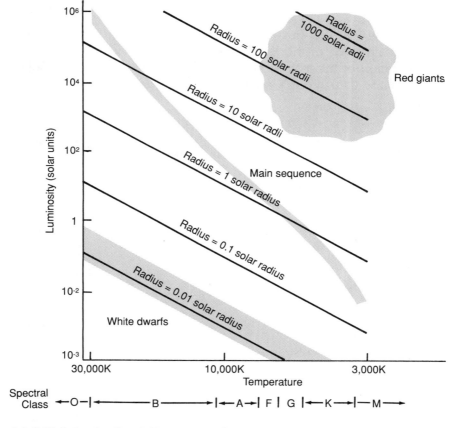

F I G U R E   6 . 2 A Hertzsprung-Russell diagram, showing where stars of different sizes are found. The largest stars are the *red giants*, in the upper right corner, and the smallest are the *white dwarfs* in the lower left. The *main sequence*, consisting of stars comparable in size to the sun, is in the middle. (*Source:* Shipman, Harry L. *The Restless Universe.* Copyright © 1979 by Houghton Mifflin Company, p. 237. Used with permission.)

CONTENT ACTIVITY: LECTURE

As you listen to the lectures on the evolution of stars, take notes on what you hear. After each of the lectures, review your notes with your group members. After you have reviewed the notes, write the study questions that your teacher assigns.

ACTIVITY 4

Now that you have reviewed all your notes in your group, outline the main ideas of the lecture in the space provided. Focus on the organization of the lecture rather than on details. Choose a spokesperson to share your group's outline with the class.

Lecture Review Outline

I. Introduction

II. Classifying Stars

III. Star Deaths

SKILL FOCUS ACTIVITY

ACTIVITY 5

Classifying

To classify is to sort members of a group into categories whose members share particular characteristics. Given the enormous number of objects of study in any field, advances in science depend on the accurate classification of data. In the lecture, you learned that stars can be classified according to their luminosity, temperature, and size. The number of classes of stars is infinite, but astronomers have agreed on certain parameters to define members of groups. By studying typical members of each group, scientists can learn more about the whole group. Intense study of our sun, for example, helped them learn about main sequence stars. Classification, then, is an important step in the process of scientific inquiry.

As a student, you will be required to organize information by classification. To help you develop skills in ordering elements, with your group members, choose one of the following topics, and prepare a presentation. Follow these steps:

1. Observe and study the elements in the group. Look for similarities and differences among their properties.

2. Decide on what property or combination of properties you wish to use in your selection of subgroups.

3. Divide the elements into subgroups.

4. Study the subgroups. Look for significant patterns that are typical of all members of the subgroup and that exclude members of other subgroups.

5. Prepare your presentation. Describe your subgroups in terms of the property or combination of properties you chose as your criteria for selection.

TOPICS

1. Current student population of the class. (Interview students.)
2. Businesses on a main street or in an area of the city or town in which you live.
3. Books and magazines read by students in the class in the last month.
4. Class activities in an English-language program.

HELPFUL VOCABULARY

The criteria we used for selection were _____.

We found similarities in _____.

We found differences in _____.

This subgroup includes _____.

All members of this group _____.

CONTENT ACTIVITIES: READING

ACTIVITY 6

Reading Preview Questions

Answer the following questions *before* beginning to read "Galaxies and Clusters."

1. What is the main idea of this reading? (Check the title and subtitles, look for illustrations, and read the first and last paragraphs to find main ideas.)

2. What do you already know about this topic? Make a quick list of ideas or words that come to mind.

3. Read the questions that follow the reading and look for the answers as you read.

Now read the following passage.

Galaxies and Clusters
Hyron Spinrad
University of California, Berkeley

Galaxies — vast collections of billions of stars — are the basic building blocks of the universe. These grand objects are so enormous in size that they simply dwarf all human experience. The amount of light and other energies they give off defy any attempt at everyday comparison. Yet, since we confirmed the existence of other galaxies in the 1920's, telescopes of increasing power and sophistication have shown us not just a few, not hundreds or thousands, but hundreds of billions of these grand star systems in every direction we look.

Galaxies also turn out to be "gregarious" — they generally do not appear to live alone. We find them gathered together in smaller groups or larger clusters, and those groups and clusters themselves tend to join together in immense structures astronomers call *superclusters*. Figure [6.3] is a photograph that I took at the Cerro Tololo Interamerican Observatory in Chile, where a 4-meter (158-inch) diameter telescope sits atop a peak in the Andes and affords astronomers beautifully clear views of the night sky. The photograph shows a rich cluster of galaxies unromantically called Str 0431-616 (a name derived from its position in the sky). This impressive collection of galaxies is visible only from the Earth's Southern Hemisphere, by the way. As you look at the picture, keep in mind that each object that is elongated (rather than just a point) on this image is a galaxy of stars.

Furthermore, . . . we have also discovered that the universe of galaxies is rapidly expanding on the largest scale. All the galaxies are receding from one another, so that in the time it has taken you to read this page, the distance to the cluster of galaxies shown in Figure [6.3] has opened up by another full million miles! This expansion is a fundamental feature of the universe which illuminates and is illuminated by our study of galaxies.

Spiral galaxies, like our own Milky Way, are most common in the universe, but as we will see, galaxies can show other shapes as well. A spiral galaxy is a huge spinning Frisbee-shaped agglomeration of stars, gas, and dust — all held together by the mutual attraction of gravity. The flat disk of a typical spiral is about 60,000 light-years in diameter — which means that communication from one edge to the other would take at least 60,000 years. Actually, the edges of spiral galaxies like our own are somewhat poorly defined; we can see where the visible material begins to thin out, but we have been accumulating a great deal of indirect evidence that the galaxy continues much farther outward than its visible edges, and generally contains much more material than we presently have the technology to see. Recently, physicists have begun to speculate that this material may be in the form of exotic subatomic particles that our theories may predict but which we have not yet discovered in our laboratories. . . . Here we should merely note how amazing it is that even at this writing — late in the twentieth century — astronomers and physicists still need to worry that our census of the basic constituents of galaxies could be seriously deficient.

Let us confine our attention, then, to the material in galaxies that we can detect with our present-day instruments. If we were to examine a representative spiral galaxy, we would find that it contains upward of 100 billion stars in its vast pinwheel. In addition, perhaps 10 percent of its material is uncondensed gas and dust — the raw material of the universe — sprinkled among the stars and generally confined to the galaxy's main disk. Figure [6.4] shows a beautiful example of a spiral galaxy, called NGC 891, seen with its disk edge-on to us. In this view, the band directly across the main disk of the galaxy is a vast lane of dust.

This might be a good time to say something about the way galaxies are named by astronomers. Except for our nearest neighbor galaxies, there are far too many of these star systems to give each of them a name. Thus, astronomers designate them by their numbers in various important catalogues of galaxies that have been drawn up over the years. The most common of these, the *New General Catalogue of Nebulae and Clusters of Stars* (or *NGC*), was published by astronomer J. L. E. Dreyer in 1888. (Although the catalogue includes many galaxies, the title does not mention that category because in Dreyer's day galaxies were still confused with nebulae.)

Another main type of galaxy is the elliptical or E galaxy, whose general shape is like a slightly elongated basketball or football. When we see a three-dimensional object like this projected on the sky, it

FIGURE 6.3 The rich and concentrated cluster of galaxies Str 0431-616.

FIGURE 6.4 The nearby spiral galaxy NGC 891, seen edge-on.

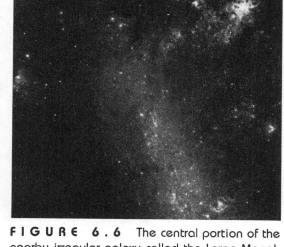

FIGURE 6.5 The galaxy NGC 3115, an O type, seen edge-on.

urce: Photos courtesy Hyron Spinrad.

FIGURE 6.6 The central portion of the nearby irregular galaxy called the Large Magellanic Cloud.

appears to us to be shaped like an ellipse. These E galaxies turn out to be the most common in clusters or groups of galaxies. Most E galaxies are smooth-looking objects on long-exposure photographs. The light of the stars blends together and it takes hard work to measure the properties of the constituent stars individually. These galaxies contain less raw material—interstellar gas and dust—than do the spirals. There is an intermediate type of galaxy, called an SO, which looks rather like an elliptical one, but does show an underlying disk structure. Figure [6.5] shows NGC 3115, and edge-on smooth SO galaxy. What you see is a smooth blending of starlight in the image and a lack of interstellar matter. In the cluster shown in Figure [6.3], the larger galaxies are mainly ellipticals and SOs, pretty crowded together near the cluster center and thinning out toward its periphery.

Not all galaxies show a regular structure: Some have a more chaotic shape or no well-defined shape at all, and are thus called *irregulars*. Figure [6.6] shows a detailed view of such a galaxy: one of our nearest neighbors, the Large Magellanic Cloud. Because this galaxy is so close—at 150,000 light-years it is a "satellite" of our Milky Way—a lot of individual stars can be seen in the photograph.

Whatever a galaxy's type, astronomers have discovered that there is a complex relationship between the stars and the raw material. This is because new stars are born from the gas and dust in a galaxy, and stars at the end of their lives often return some of their material to the galactic reservoir. The returned material has frequently been "processed" by the star and now consists of a greater proportion of heavier elements. One of the great realizations of twentieth-century astronomy is that the shape and other large-scale properties of galaxies are intimately intertwined with the "ecology" of the stars—their interactions with their environment. In fact, recent evidence indicates that even within immense clusters of galaxies, environmental interactions may play a role in determining the properties of the individual galaxies. (More on this idea in a moment.) . . .

CLUSTERS OF GALAXIES

If you ask an amateur astronomer in which direction in the sky you can see the largest number of galaxies with a small telescope, the answer you will get is the constellation Virgo. This is because the section of the sky we call Virgo contains a relatively nearby and fairly rich cluster of galaxies. (In the extragalactic vastness, the distance to the Virgo cluster—some 50 million light-years—doesn't seem all that large!) In fact, it turns out that our Milky Way, the Andromeda galaxy, and the rest of our small "Local Group" of galaxies are outriders of the Virgo cluster—or, to put it more properly, our group is part of the Virgo *supercluster* of galaxies. This larger ensemble contains several straggly clusters of galaxies, held together even across intergalactic distances by gravity's unrelenting pull. Recent measurements indicate that our Local Group is being pulled toward the Virgo cluster at a speed of about 150 miles *per second*.

Astronomers have devised some arbitrary definitions for grouping galaxies: A *binary galaxy pair* is two clearly related galaxies, a *group* is between five and 25 galaxies within a space of some 2 to 4 million light-years, and a *cluster* is a single collection with more galaxies spread out over a larger volume. A conglomeration of several groups and clusters is then called a *supercluster*.

The late astronomer George Abell of UCLA compiled an important catalogue of galaxy clusters. The rich clusters he lists can contain anywhere from one hundred to several thousand luminous galaxies in a volume of about ten million light-years. The largest superclusters could contain as many as 20,000 galaxies over vast distances. A stringy filament of galaxies winding through the constellations of Perseus and Pegasus, for example, is about a billion light-years in length!

Like collections of people, galaxy groups and clusters are often dominated by one or several large members. In our Local Group, for example, there are two obvious leaders in size and mass: our Milky Way and the Andromeda spiral. Next in line is the Triangulum galaxy, M33, and then the Large Magellanic Cloud we discussed earlier. The other more numerous members of our group are medium-size irregulars and some small ellipticals. We have no large E galaxy near us; this is a pity, because we would very much have liked to study one of these imposing galaxies from a closer perspective.

The rich clusters of galaxies may be loose and ragged-looking or they may show a more concentrated and symmetric appearance, like the one shown in Figure [6.3]. While the loose clusters generally contain both spirals and ellipticals, the denser, more concentrated clusters have more large E galaxies than spirals, at least near their centers.

In the same way that we can use the motions within a galaxy to measure its total mass, we can use the motions of galaxies within a cluster to get an indication of the total mass the cluster contains. (This sounds easy in principle, but can be quite challenging in practice, since we must measure Doppler shifts in the faint light of several very distant objects. The electronic technology of the 1980's has been a great help in "amplifying" small amounts of light, just as your stereo receiver at home can amplify the faint signals coming from your turntable.)

The masses we derive for various clusters turn out to be about ten times larger than we anticipated from our present knowledge of the masses of individual spiral and elliptical galaxies. Once again, our observations seem to be telling us that there is an embarrassingly large "missing mass" — some other major constituent that is invisible to us.

ACTIVITY 7

Using information from the reading, answer the following questions.

Reading Questions

1. What are the common characteristics of galaxies?

2. List the types of galaxies and their distinguishing characteristics. Which is most common?

3. What do astronomers hypothesize and/or know about the composition of galaxies?

4. Within what galaxy is the earth? To which group(s) does our galaxy belong?

ACTIVITY 8

In your groups, discuss the following problem. Use your answers from the reading questions to help you. Choose a spokesperson to report your group's answer to the class.

Reading Discussion Problem

An unidentified celestial object has been found. Astronomers suspect it to be a previously unknown galaxy. Outline the steps you, as an astronomer, might take to classify this object as a galaxy.

SKILL FOCUS ACTIVITY

ACTIVITY 9

Forming Hypotheses

Hypotheses are provisional explanations of *situations* we have observed. Hypotheses must be tested with *evidence* to determine if they are true or not.

EXAMPLE

Scientists had theorized that one result of a supernova explosion was the formation of a neutron star. Neutron stars were formed, they hypothesized, during the catastrophic collapse of a massive star. As the star's core collapses, there is an increase in its rotation and magnetic field. Scientists, however, lacked any evidence that neutron stars even existed.

Situation A graduate student discovered regularly spaced bursts of radio pulses coming from a celestial object. Other scientists spotted optical pulses coming from the same object.

Hypothesis To explain this discovery, astronomers developed the hypothesis that the source of these bursts was electromagnetic radiation being emitted by a rotating neutron star, which they named "pulsar."

Evidence The astronomers discovered that the rapid pulse rate of these objects slowed down just a little, which meant that the rotating object was losing energy. The amount of energy lost was just enough to supply enough energy to make the clouds of gas, surrounding the pulsar, glow. The amount of energy lost depends on the nature of the spinning object.

Conclusion Therefore, the scientists concluded, the source of the pulses must be a neutron star, whose axis is tilted with respect to its magnetic pole. As the star spins, it turns on its axis and a beam of electromagnetic radiation escapes near the magnetic poles, causing it to appear, from our position on earth, to pulse. If the spinning star were not a neutron star, it would supply too much energy to the glowing gas, which would conflict with what was observed.

This process of hypothesis testing is an integral part of scientific inquiry. Following are three situations. In your groups, create hypotheses to explain the situations, provide evidence to support or validate the hypotheses, and state a conclusion. Choose a spokesperson from your group to present your investigation to the class.

1. An employee received a commendation letter from his supervisor last week. In the letter, the supervisor praised the employee's work and leadership on the last project that the employee's unit had completed. The employee appears not to be working very hard on his or her unit's present project.

2. Floods from the local river have been more frequent in town X during the past five years since a dam was completed 15 miles north of the town. It was built to generate electricity for the area and to aid in irrigation for the expanding vegetable farms north of the town. The area had suffered a three-year drought prior to the dam's construction.

3. The population of city B has decreased steadily for the past two decades despite no decline in the birth rate. In the last ten years the city has lost its automobile manufacturing plants, which moved south, but it has been successful in attracting several major banks to set up headquarters in the city.

HELPFUL VOCABULARY

We hypothesize that _____.

It is possible that _____.

We might infer from the evidence that _____.

The evidence points to _____.

The evidence supports the conclusion that _____.

EVALUATION ACTIVITIES

ACTIVITY 10

Test Review

Your teacher will distribute the study questions that your class wrote for this unit. In your groups, review your notes to make sure you have the information to answer the questions.

ACTIVITY 11

Test Correction

In your groups, review your answers to the test questions. If an answer is wrong, try to determine why and then try to find the correct answer. If you cannot figure out why an answer is wrong, ask your teacher for assistance.

ACTIVITY 12

Feedback Questionnaire

Answer the following questions concerning your experience working in your group. Be as explicit as you can. Only your teacher will read your answers, but you will be asked if you would like to share some of your answers in a class discussion.

1. What kind of communication problems did your group encounter during the unit? How did you solve the problems?

2. Were all of your group members in class every day? What happened to the group if someone was absent? What happened to the absentee group member when he or she came back?

3. Did your group usually stay on task? If not, what happened?

4. Did you group have a leader? What was the effect on the group of having a leader or of not having a leader?

5. What problems did your group encounter related to cultural differences? How did you solve the problems?

6. What did you learn about group dynamics from working in your group? What did you learn about yourself?

7. How did you contribute to the success or failure of your group?

8. What were some of the advantages of working in your group? What were some of the disadvantages?

9. What plans do you have to change your behavior in your next group? How will this change help you learn English better?

10. What suggestions do you have to give your teacher concerning the activities that your group completed in this unit?

UNIT
SEVEN

American
Political
Culture

PREVIEW ACTIVITIES

Your teacher will divide your class into groups. These groups will remain the same throughout the unit.

A C T I V I T Y 1

In your groups, discuss the following questions. Gather as many answers as possible from group members. Choose a spokesperson to report your ideas to the class.

Preview Discussion

1. Describe your country's form of government and election processes. How long has your country had this form of government? How did it come into existence?

2. What is the racial, religious, and national make-up of your country's population? How do different national, racial, and religious groups correspond to class groups in your culture?

3. In your country, what are your civil rights as an individual? What are your civil responsibilities?

4. Do you consider your country to be democratic? Why?

5. Define *democracy*.

A C T I V I T Y 2

In your groups, try to determine the meanings of the following words. Do not use a dictionary. You will be comparing your definitions with those of the other groups, so take notes during your discussion. Choose a spokesperson to report your definitions to the class.

Lecture Vocabulary

1. preconception
2. "on a short leash"
3. stable
4. legitimacy
5. "in a fish bowl"
6. impinge
7. affluence
8. nobility
9. persecution
10. scarcity
11. serfs
12. preserve (v)
13. negotiate
14. compromise (v)
15. accountable

CONTENT ACTIVITY: LECTURE

As you listen to the lectures on American political culture, take notes on what you hear. After each of the lectures, review your notes with your group members. After you have reviewed the notes, write the study questions that your teacher assigns.

A C T I V I T Y 3

Now that you have reviewed all your notes, in your group, outline the main ideas of the lecture in the space provided. Focus on the organization of the lecture rather than on details. Choose a spokesperson to share your outline with the class.

Lecture Review Outline

I.

CONTENT ACTIVITIES: READING

ACTIVITY 4

Answer the following questions *before* beginning to read "Affirmative Action."

Reading Preview Questions

1. What is the main idea of this textbook reading? (Check the title and subtitles, look for illustrations, and read the first and last paragraphs to find main ideas.)

2. What do you already know about this topic? Make a quick list of ideas or words that come to mind.

3. Read the questions that follow the reading, and look for the answers as you read.

Now read the following passage.

Affirmative Action

During the 1970s, the United States experienced a new debate about citizenship. Like the debates that preceded it, this one is about equality. The catch phrase **"affirmative action"** is at the center of the debate. Crudely stated, affirmative action was thought to be reverse discrimination. *It is intended to discriminate on behalf of those who have been discriminated against in the past.*

We can best understand the dynamics of affirmative action by concentrating on racial equality, though the logic of affirmative action is also applicable to sex discrimination, age discrimination, or any other form of discrimination.

Affirmative action emerged during the 1970s, following a decade in which civil rights activity had lessened some forms of racial discrimination: blacks and other minorities were no longer systematically excluded from the rights of citizenship, such as voting or holding office. And they were no longer legally excluded from jobs, housing, good schools, restaurants, and baseball teams.

However, this social transformation failed to accomplish two important things. It has not ended segregation, and it has not ended severe economic inequalities between black and white citizens. For example, in Chicago, the public schools are 70 percent nonwhite; in Baltimore, the figure is 75 percent; in Detroit, 81 percent; and in Washington, D.C., 96 percent. Persistent segregation is accompanied by persistent economic inequality. The 1970 census was taken at the end of a decade that gave a lot of attention to racial justice — more books were written, more meetings held, more marches organized, more legislation passed, more programs started, more commissions

Source: Excerpt (pages 150–152) from *An Introduction to American Government,* 4/e, by Kenneth Prewitt and Sidney Verba. Copyright ©1983 by Kenneth Prewitt and Sidney Verba. Reprinted by permission of Harper & Row, Publishers, Inc.

formed, more money spent on solving "the American dilemma" than in any other period of our history. At the end of that decade, the median income of white families was $9,961 whereas for black families it was $6,067.

It was out of frustration with the persistence of segregation and inequality that the drive for affirmative action arose. Ending discrimination did not correct the lingering effects of past discrimination: inferior schools, urban ghetto living, poverty, and broken homes. And initiatives in the private sector produced little more than tokenism.

At this point, the actions of government began to force society to abandon the principle of colorblindness. The civil rights movement of the 1960s sought to make the law colorblind, to rid the law and society of a tradition of discrimination. The affirmative-action movement of the 1970s sought to again make the law take race into account. The principles of affirmative action were also applied in order to compensate for sex discrimination. According to the idea of reverse discrimination, it is the "haves" who will be inconvenienced, and even discriminated against, so that the "have-nots," especially blacks, native Americans, Mexican Americans, and Puerto Ricans, can have a better chance at the good schools and the good jobs that will produce economic equality with whites. Similar efforts have been made to improve the status of women.

The language of affirmative action is that of "targets," "goals," or "quotas." If the outcome of college admission procedures or employment and promotion practices is not proportional to the representation of racial minorities in the population, this is taken as evidence that discrimination lingers. Guidelines are then suggested for the college or the business, with the threat that federal moneys may be withdrawn or other penalties imposed if the target figure is not reached.

Implicit in affirmative-action programs was the shift from equality of opportunity to equality of condition. The success of a college admissions program is not measured by whether it gives everyone an equal chance at admission but whether it achieves a certain outcome. Given past discrimination, a colorblind admissions program will probably result in very few blacks being qualified for college entrance. Only if the college takes color into account and attempts to meet some quota is it likely to enroll a large number of blacks.

Affirmative action as government policy is deeply troubling to many citizens. It moves beyond equal protection of the law and even beyond equal opportunity to a new concept of citizen rights: the right to be treated unequally, though favorably, in compensation for previous unequal and unfavorable treatment.

Such treatment cannot avoid being called reverse discrimination. Groups that have struggled to succeed under the old rules resent the change in the rules that would seem to penalize them just because they are white or male.

A C T I V I T Y 5

Using information from the reading, answer the following questions.

Reading Questions

1. What does *affirmative action*, *tokenism*, and *colorblind* mean?

2. What led to the development of affirmative-action policies?

3. What is the purpose of affirmative action?

4. What do the authors suggest about the relationship between equality and affirmative action?

ACTIVITY 6

In your groups, discuss the following questions. Use your answers from the reading questions to help you answer them. Choose a spokesperson to report your answers to the class

Reading Discussion Questions

1. What arguments would you give for affirmative action?

2. What arguments would you give against affirmative action?

3. How does the concept of affirmative action reflect the American political belief system?

SKILL FOCUS ACTIVITY

ACTIVITY 7

Interpreting Poll Data

Social scientists, particularly political scientists, do extensive research on public attitudes. This research gives them insights into how Americans think about all kinds of issues. One technique used to carry out this research is polling, asking members of the public or of specific groups what they think about a particular issue or event. The poll usually consists of a question or series of related questions and pre-determined answer choices. Respondents (those who participate in the polls) select the answer that is closest to their own views. There are several national polling organizations (Gallup and Harris, for example) whose poll results appear weekly in such magazines as *Time* and *Newsweek*.

Poll results have numerous uses. They may determine whether candidates run for office. If candidates run, poll data are used to tell them how they should run their campaigns. The Nielsen polls tell television producers which shows Americans like to watch and which programs Americans do not enjoy. Shows that do not get high Nielsen ratings are often cancelled. Academic texts and lectures will often use poll data to support arguments or viewpoints. As a student, you must become familiar with the format and use of poll data. You must also learn how to interpret polls and how to report poll results.

Following are some of the questions and poll results from surveys on American political attitudes. Discuss the questions and results with your group. Try to discover the issue, idea, or value each question is attempting to survey, and then draw some conclusions about the answers. Choose a spokesperson to present your analysis and conclusions to the class.

P O L L   1   Public Attitudes on Affirmative Action

"The government should see to it that people who have been discriminated against in the past get a better break in the future."

Whites		Blacks	
Agree	68%	Agree	85%
Disagree	25%	Disagree	9%

"First of all, would you approve or disapprove of requiring businesses to hire a certain number of minority workers?"

Whites		Blacks	
Approve	35%	Approve	64%
Disapprove	60%	Disapprove	26%

"What about a college or graduate school giving special consideration to the best minority applicants, to help more of them get admitted than otherwise. Would you approve or disapprove of that?"

Whites		Blacks	
Approve	59%	Approve	83%
Disapprove	36%	Disapprove	16%

P O L L   1   (Continued)

"How about requiring large companies to set up special training programs for members of minority groups?"

Whites		Blacks	
Approve	63%	Approve	88%
Disapprove	32%	Disapprove	9%

"What if a school reserved a certain number of places for qualified minority applicants. Would you approve or disapprove of that even if it meant that some qualified white applicants wouldn't be admitted?"

Whites		Blacks	
Approve	32%	Approve	46%
Disapprove	60%	Disapprove	42%

Source: Lipset, Seymour Martin and William Schneider, "The Bakke Case: How Would It Be Decided at the Bar of Public Opinion," *Public Opinion*, March/April, 1978, p. 42. Reprinted with the permission of the American Enterprise for Public Policy Research.

P O L L   2   Opposition to Libertarian Values among Opinion Leaders and the General Public

	GENERAL PUBLIC (N = 938)	OPINION LEADERS (N = 845)
1. Our laws should aim to:		
• Protect a citizen's right to live by any moral standards he chooses	23	33
• Enforce the community's standards of right and wrong	55	34
• Decline to choose	23	33
2. Which of these comes closer to your own view?		
• Nobody has the right to decide what should or should not be published	29	51
• To protect its moral values, a society sometimes has to forbid certain things from being published	54	33
• Decline to choose	17	16

3. A newspaper has a right to publish its opinions:

• No matter how false and twisted its opinions are	9	31
• Only if it doesn't twist the facts and tell lies	81	57
• Decline to choose	10	12

Source: Opinions and Values of Americans Survey, 1975–77, in McClosky, Herbert and John Zaller, *The American Ethos: Public Attitudes Toward Capitalism and Democracy* (Cambridge, Massachusetts: Harvard University Press), p. 39. Reprinted by permission. Copyright © 1985 by the President and Fellows of Harvard College.

DEFINITIONS

Opinion leaders—politically active or influential Americans: party leaders, activists, reporters and columnists, leaders in education, labor and so on.

General public—American people who are not politically active or influential

N—the number of persons polled

HELPFUL VOCABULARY

The question is polling attitudes about _____.

_____ percent of _____ support (oppose) _____.

These data suggest that _____.

If you compare the responses in question _____ to those in question _____, then _____.

There is not much difference in the percentage of _____ and _____.

_____ and _____ are surprisingly similar (different) in their views on _____.

PROBLEM-SOLVING ACTIVITY

ACTIVITY 8

Polling Activity

In your group, select three or four questions from the preceding surveys and poll your fellow foreign students. Make your inquiry anonymous. Compare your results with those of the Americans surveyed in the original study. Summarize your group's conclusions, and choose a spokesperson to present the conclusions to the class.

SKILL FOCUS ACTIVITY

ACTIVITY 9

Presenting and Defending Opinions

As a student, you will be called on to present your ideas and opinions and defend them against the questions and arguments of others. The person who successfully persuades others to accept his or her viewpoint or who wins an argument or a debate has a well-thought-through opinion with the facts to prove it. He or she also knows the counterargument (the argument against his or her viewpoint or reasons) and the facts that support it. As John Stuart Mill, a famous British philosopher, said, "He who knows only his own position, knows little of that."

To support your viewpoint in an academic setting, you should use reasons supported by facts, references to authority, clear examples, and objective answers to the counterarguments. Reasons that appeal only to emotions are not acceptable in an academic setting.

Read the following two paragraphs, and in your group, analyze the arguments. For what is the paragraph arguing? What is the counterargument? What reasons does the author give to support his argument? How does the author support these reasons? Choose a spokesperson to report your group's analysis to the class.

The rich should pay a higher proportion of their income in taxes so that government can provide greater social insurance and welfare to the middle class, the working class, and the poor. People should not have to do without necessities, such as adequate housing, food, and health care, while the rich purchase luxuries, such as jewelry, expensive cars, second homes, and lavish entertainment and vacations. Although some claim that a larger welfare state in the United States would weaken incentives and hurt economic growth, OECD* data show that in Sweden, where the rich are taxed more heavily than they are in the United States and government social programs are a much bigger part of the Swedish economy, the rate of economic growth has been substantially greater than in the United States. Greater equality has not hurt efficiency. Having government invest in the well-being of the workforce, and giving people confidence in their future and satisfaction with society's fairness, may actually have increased efficiency in Sweden.

The rich should not pay a higher proportion of their income in taxes so that government can provide greater social insurance and welfare to the middle class, the working class, and the poor. A bigger welfare state will lead to lower economic growth and a slower rise in everyone's standard of living. Expanded government social programs weaken incentives to work and to save, leading to slower economic growth. By taxing the rich to pay for these programs, saving and investment are reduced, which also hurts economic growth because the rich, having higher incomes, save more and invest more. Supporters of increased taxes on the rich cite Sweden as an example of a country with a large welfare state, a rising rate of economic growth, and higher taxes on the rich. In Sweden, however, tax rates on all citizens are higher than in the United States, not just taxes on the rich. Because Swedish culture is different from American culture—incentives and institutions work differently in Sweden than in the United States—there is no guarantee that adopting the Swedish model will produce similar economic growth in the United States.

HELPFUL VOCABULARY

_____ should (must) _____.

I think _____.

I would argue that _____.

There is (other) evidence to show that _____.

I disagree because _____.

*Organization for Economic Cooperation and Development

If it is the case that _____, then _____.

It follows that _____.

_____ implies that _____.

The best proof is _____.

ACTIVITY 10

In your groups, choose one of the following opinions and prepare arguments to support it. Be sure to make the argument academic rather than emotional. Choose a spokesperson to present your group's argument to the class.

OPINIONS

1. Work is the single most important determinant of social status.
2. Work plays a fundamental role in the formation of self-esteem.
3. The community should protect children from ideas it considers wrong and dangerous.
4. A proper education includes free discussion of all ideas and subjects.
5. Encouraging immigration from less developed countries is the best way to solve the problems of an aging workforce.
6. Affirmative-action programs are necessary to create real equal opportunity for minorities.

EVALUATION ACTIVITIES

ACTIVITY 11

Test Review

Your teacher will distribute the study questions that your class wrote for this unit. In your groups, review your notes to make sure you have the information to answer the questions.

ACTIVITY 12

Test Correction

In your groups, review your answers to the test questions. If an answer is wrong, try to determine why it is wrong and then try to find the correct answer. If you cannot determine why an answer is wrong, ask your teacher for assistance.

ACTIVITY 13

Scenarios

Each group will receive one copy of a scenario role, and your group will have 10 to 15 minutes to prepare for this activity.

ACTIVITY 14

After your class has rehearsed, performed, and discussed the scenarios, complete the following exercise.

Student Scenario Worksheet

1. *Vocabulary and idioms:* Write here as many of the new words as you can remember from today's scenarios.

2. *Topic and roles:* What was the topic of each scenario? Write a brief description of the different roles performed by the students, and include a description of the performers' goals.

3. *Strategies:* How did the student performers try to accomplish their goals? What particular strategies were most effective? Who had the most control of the conversations? Why?

4. *Structures:* List here examples of new constructions you learned today. What grammar points are illustrated?

A C T I V I T Y 15

Answer the following questions concerning your experience working in your group. Be as explicit as you can. Only your teacher will read your answers, but you will be asked if you would like to share some of your answers in a class discussion.

Feedback Questionnaire

1. What kind of communication problems did your group encounter during the unit? How did you solve the problems?

2. Were all of your group members in class every day? What happened to the group if someone was absent? What happened to the absentee group member when he or she came back?

3. Did your group usually stay on task? If not, what happened?

4. Did your group have a leader? What was the effect on the group of having a leader or of not having a leader?

5. What problems did your group encounter that may have been related to cultural differences? How did you solve the problems?

6. What did you learn about group dynamics from working in your group? What did you learn about yourself?

7. How did you contribute to the success or failure of your group?

8. What were some of the advantages of working in this group? What were some of the disadvantages?